DIVORCE – AND AFTER

Gerald Sanctuary is a solicitor and the
Marriage Under Stress. Formerly the
of the National Marriage Gu
more recently Executive
formation and Ed
States, he has
television, and
lecturing and pa
to marriage, divorce

Constance Whitehead children,
and is herself divorced. ten extensively
as a freelance journalist wspapers, magazines
and journals about marriage and divorce and a wide
variety of other topics. For two years she was honorary press officer to the National Federation of Clubs for the Divorced and Separated. She is at present studying to qualify as a teacher.

GERALD SANCTUARY
and
CONSTANCE WHITEHEAD

Divorce – and After

PENGUIN HANDBOOK

Penguin Books Ltd, Harmondsworth, Middlesex, England
Penguin Books Inc., 7110 Ambassador Road, Baltimore, Maryland 21207, U.S.A.
Penguin Books Australia Ltd, Ringwood, Victoria, Australia

—

First published by Victor Gollancz 1970
Published in Penguin Books 1972

—

—

Made and printed in Great Britain
by C. Nicholls & Company Ltd
Set in Linotype Granjon

Contents

CHAPTER I

People, Problems and Feelings

DIVORCE: the word we use to mean the legal ending of a marriage. In fact it means a lot more than that. It represents the end of the hopes of two people, the certificate that their relationship did not endure. Divorce is not just a matter of law. It concerns people under stress, and our society has not yet learned to understand them.

We are not concerned here to discuss rights and wrongs, nor to point morals. We believe that the majority of divorced and separated people find themselves in a thoroughly unpleasant situation with little idea of how to cope with it. The best that can be said is that there is an increasing body of experience of what it is like to become divorced and of the kind of life that has to be led by people living alone after the end of their marriage or bringing up children on their own. Over 100,000 people are divorced each year, and this figure has been rising for more than ten years.

Nothing we can say will make the situation pleasant. This is one of the main messages of this book. At the same time, we can help you to see the situation for what it is; we can show how it is possible to re-create a life of meaning from what seemed to be total disaster; and we can give in detail the various ways in which support can be found.

We should like to start by trying to sort out the facts that are part of the situation from the feelings that go with them. This is not easy. Let us take Mrs A as an example: she was deserted by her husband six months ago, and is left to manage their home and their two children, a boy of seven and a girl of five. Mr A is still sending her some money, but she has no idea how long he will go on doing this, and anyway it is not enough. She has to try to answer the children's questions, pay the bills, clean the house, do the shopping, face the neighbours and explain things to her parents. She finds herself bursting into tears at moments when she needs to be able to retain some kind of calm, and when she is alone she sits as though in a daze, unable to do the work that is piling up all round her.

Mrs A has decided that her husband is not coming back. She thinks she had better get a divorce, but she seems incapable of doing anything about it. Her mother tells her she should make a 'clean break', and friends have offered to look after the children if she wants to go out. Several bills are unpaid, and she worries about the children having new clothes and some kind of holiday in the summer.

The first way to help her is to begin to disentangle the facts and the feelings about the break-up of her marriage. What are the facts? She has not got enough money, the children need clothes, she is losing weight and is not well. But she has been offered help, she has some legal rights which can be enforced, she was trained as a skilled telephonist and could take this up again. There are other facts, of course, but these are enough to start with. What are Mrs A's feelings about all this? We know she is miserable, and although she is entitled to a divorce (Mr A admits he has been unfaithful) she cannot bring herself to think about it yet. This may sound strange, because we know that she has already decided that she should divorce her husband. So why doesn't she go ahead and see a solicitor? She does not do this because she has two different feelings that conflict with one another. She bitterly resents what she feels Mr A has done to her, thinks he should be punished for it, and that she should be allowed her freedom from a marriage that was a mistake from the beginning. On the other hand, the idea of visiting a lawyer appals her. She cannot face the prospect of having to tell the whole story to a stranger.

Mrs A has other conflicting feelings; she thinks that Mr A should be kept away from the children after what he has done to her; but at the same time she believes that they ought to see their father. She would not take him back, but thinks he needs looking after. If he comes looking more cheerful than usual she feels it unfair that he should be enjoying himself while she has so much worry and responsibility. Then there are the children; she clings to them as the only real people in her life, yet finds herself shouting at them for leaving their clothes all over the floor. And so on.

What about Mr A? We are not making the assumption that women need help whereas men can help themselves. On the contrary, many men find it even more difficult to manage life on their own. Neither are we taking the attitude that it is always the wife who is long-suffering and the husband who is the villain. We are concerned to offer help where it is needed, or to show how it can be obtained.

So Mr A has problems. If you asked him, he would say that he was fully justified in leaving his wife, though his anxiety to prove it to you suggests that he also feels guilty. He feels she is asking continually for money which he can ill afford to pay her. He is desperately worried about money, and about the cost of legal proceedings, should she decide to bring them against him, though at the same time he wishes she would stop dithering and get on with it. He has never dealt with solicitors, and oddly enough his fears about them are similar to those of Mrs A. He has trouble washing clothes and buying food, and finds he has largely lost contact with his family. He tends to drift from situation to situation, club to club, not knowing where he is going or even where he wants to go. He meets several women and has had one or two brief affairs, but these have seemed only to make him more lonely. He, too, is confused and needs help.

He needs information about his legal rights and responsibilities and he also will probably be wise to get medical advice. There might be ways in which he could expand his interests in a less aimless way. He can be advised about his diet, and helped with the problem of getting his laundry done and of buying the things that he needs. In addition to practical help, he may also need support concerning his conflicting emotional problems, the use of his sexuality, and his feelings of guilt.

There is nothing unusual about having feelings that conflict with one another. This is something that many people do not realize. Feelings are seldom rational and in a situation like this they are bound to clash in an irrational way. Feelings however, do not alter facts. So far as money problems are concerned, Mrs A can get help, and can enforce her legal rights. The Department of Health and Social Security – as its name implies – exists to help women in her position, and a lawyer will be able to act on her behalf, possibly without any cost to her at all. There may be ways of obtaining clothes for the children, if she knows where to ask. As far as her depression is concerned, her doctor will certainly be able to help her.

You will notice that we have not said that there are instant, easy or effortless ways of solving people's problems, least of all their emotional ones. Consider what has happened: a divorced couple's marriage has gone through degrees of stress that proved intolerable for one or both partners. And it happens slowly. There have been weeks, months, perhaps years of uncertainty and lack of sympathy. Time and time again there has been optimism followed by defeat. Things go better for a while, you think you must have imagined the crisis. It must have been due to that illness she had, to the children – all so young at the same time, to the house that was too small, to the in-laws, the lack of money, your own inexperience. It can all be forgotten or neatly rationalized now it is safely past. You begin to feel secure. And then there is another crisis. Promises are broken, resolutions forgotten, trust betrayed. Suddenly, you are further apart than ever, lonely beyond belief.

Some people have violent quarrels that grow more and more bitter as time goes on. Others have, as it were, fighting positions from which they more subtly destroy one another. There is the husband who, lacking confidence himself, criticizes and complains of what he feels are his wife's inadequacies. She, deeply distressed, starts *trying* to please him. Anxiously she wonders, watches his eyes, waits for the verdict. If it is good, maybe she shows her relief, and in doing so lets him see how justified were his doubts. Failed after all, instead of reassuring her, he can only respond with coldness, suspicion or a sneer, and she hides her hurt with something equally clumsy and inappropriate. It is not really a quarrel, but more a deadly tightening of tension, another twist in the distorting forms of two characters interacting disastrously on one another.

Next time she tries harder, he sees her ineptitude more plainly and finds it more infuriating. Exposed and hurt again, she starts to feel that whatever she says or does will be wrong. Unless the chain of reactions can be broken and the husband and wife can become aware of what they are doing and helped to stop doing it, one or other may well make a bid for what looks like freedom. The kind of loneliness this sort of situation brings is unendurable to many people, and by others endured only at ruinous cost.

Whichever you are, the one who left or the one who stayed, you probably wish for all you are worth that everyone else knew and understood what has happened. For how do you tell them? And what are they going to say when you do? They were 'our' friends, 'our' relatives, 'our' doctor, milkman, bank manager. And our children. Whose are they now? Mine? Yours? And who are we – separately?

Mr and Mrs B could well be the couple we spoke of earlier who were slowly destroying each other's confidence. It was a terrible relationship; she became more and more strained and self-conscious in an effort to make her husband happy. He, depending for his happiness and self-confidence on getting definite, sympathetic responses from another person, felt more and more insecure as his wife became less and less positive. He became, in fact, cruel, without meaning to be. In an attempt to get his wife to make up her mind, say what she thought, rotate independently as a separate person instead of circulating like a satellite planet around him, he would argue with her, challenge her or try to provoke her into taking some sort of stand. This she never did for fear of being selfish or simply of saying the wrong thing. Praiseworthy perhaps, but it made a martyr of her. Listen:

He: What time shall I meet you at the station?

She: What time suits you?

He: It doesn't matter a bit.

She: Well, if I get the earlier train you won't have to put the children to bed.

He: I don't mind putting the children to bed.

She: No, but why should you? It's a bother for you. I'll get the earlier train.

He (shouting): Which train do you *want* to take?

She (almost in tears and wishing she was not going at all): The earlier one.

He, of course, has been made to feel he is being selfish, and she has indeed shortened her day's shopping so that he will not have to deal with the children. By trying not to annoy him, by making what attempt she can to see first what he wants to do so that she can fit in with this, she finds that things have only got worse. He feels that he just asked a simple question and cannot get a simple or straight answer. Neither is satisfied. And this kind of sparring happens all the time in exactly the same way, whether the issue is important or trivial.

A number of things could make this couple separate. They might part by mutual consent, unable to bear the constant warfare any longer. This is not likely, because she would find such a decision almost impossible to reach. Mr B might find another woman who could give him what he wanted. Mrs B might find another man who seemed to understand her and did not get angry. In any event, if they part, both of them, who have known such loneliness within marriage, can find themselves suddenly and surprisingly alone without it. While the marriage lasted it was a way of life – even if much of the time it felt like a life sentence. Once they separate, each will be living in a way that is oddly unfamiliar, and both will start badly undermined by doubt about the kind of people they really are. He is secretly appalled at the thought of himself as a cruel man. (She did call him cruel at the end.) She had at one time thought of herself as a reasonably clever and attractive woman. But could she be, if her husband thought her such a fool? Unkind though he undoubtedly was about it, she had to admit that she never could make decisions nowadays. These are just the kind of doubts that beset people whose marriages end in divorce. These two people, whose feelings were so violated that they could not survive together, were in spite of this so close to one another that they feel incomplete now they are apart. Violated and incomplete, each must now start working out a separate future.

Mr B, after the couple had parted, lived in lodgings. He was lonely and often bored. He drank and smoked more than he had done previously, and often felt utter despair. He wanted to see his children, and his wife made no objections. Immediately a problem arose, for where could he take four children whose ages ranged from two to eight? Driving in the car through the raw, cold winter Sundays when he took them out, they questioned him endlessly about why he had left them and where he was living. He felt cut off from them by the masses of half-truths that had to be his answers, because the whole truth was too difficult for them, and he really did not know it himself. The elder children quarrelled at intervals, the little ones cried. He got irritated with himself, and with them, and found himself out of practice at sorting them out and blowing their noses. They talked of happenings he had not shared, and school friends he did not know. It sounded as though they got on quite well without him. He wished he had a woman who could help him reach out to them. His mother? But she felt so bitter, and plainly showed her prejudice against the two children who most resembled their mother. The scenes of parting at the end of the day were frightful, Mr B already upset by his day with the children and Mrs B like an iceberg waiting to receive them. As he drove away alone into the night, his agonized mind wondered if it would be better to cut himself off from them completely. He did not know, and there was no one to ask.

He could talk to friends who were kind enough to listen, and even to offer advice, from the secure positions they occupied in life. Everyone else seemed so extremely secure. But friends behaved oddly in some ways. They seemed to search his face and his conversation as though looking for clues. It was as if they were re-assessing him in the light of his having left his wife. Some people refused to speak to him altogether, while others were almost too attentive. He felt he belonged nowhere except at work where he had always maintained a strict silence about home-life. But promotion at work had not come when he expected, so had someone told somebody else something about him that made him unsuitable – unacceptable?

Mr B's story might have been a little different if he had left his wife to live with another woman, but he would still have had to prove to himself and everyone else that the new life he was making was a success. He cannot be entirely free from doubt about his own adequacy until he has been accepted and found adequate. He still fears rejection by another woman, by his children, by his boss. In the beginning these fears are bound to be very real and to shoot up and down in size like shadows on a wall, according to his mood, his health or his luck.

Mrs B's feelings are more like Mr B's than either of them might think. Whether or not she has children, a profession, a lover, looks, money or none of these things, she too is a person whose marriage has gone wrong. Her circumstances are different from her husband's because at least she has a home. All the time it reminds her of him, and of their life together. He painted the sitting-room that colour and he wore away the arms of that chair with his hands. He is not there, but it is difficult to believe that he will not be coming back. She finds the children difficult to manage on her own, in ways that surprise her. Her subconscious plays tricks and makes dreams out of bits of the past so that when she wakes suddenly at 4 a.m. she has to think hard and painfully to remember what has happened. The children make it necessary for her to get up, but the time she goes to bed gets later and later. And why get out of the bath when there is no one waiting to get in? She has a persistent cough, and reads in a magazine that this is sometimes a sign of cancer. Could she have cancer? She cannot go to her doctor and just say 'I think I have cancer'. He would think her mad. Perhaps she is a little mad. That would account for her husband leaving her. Is she ill? She does not know, and there is no one to ask.

This applies to everything. All the official bodies who could help her have 'hours' in which they are available, and with four children she is never free enough to visit official bodies. With immense organization she can get away for a few hours. But what good is that when buses do not fit in and she may have to wait for attention? Besides, how is she to pay back the neighbours who would look after the children, and if she asks for this help now, what if there is a greater emergency later? She does not want to impose on people. Friends treat her in much the same way as they are treating her husband – either warily, or with conspicuous kindness. There are those who say 'I never really liked him', and she finds this reassuring but wonders if it is true, looking back. Others say they think he must be mad – and she says yes, she quite agrees. (Well, if *he* is, she cannot be, and that is comforting.) If she is asked out she wonders, is it done out of pity? Yet if she is not asked she feels hurt. To invite anyone to her own house requires almost superhuman effort which she simply cannot muster, besides expense which she cannot honestly afford. She is afraid of everyone and everything, yet also is on the defensive, and it takes all the running she can do to keep in the same place. Whatever friends do, however many people give her advice, information or listen to her flood of talking, in the end the doors close and she is always left alone. That is how she feels.

Mrs B loses status with the loss of her marriage. She is also worse off financially, so in both these respects she is isolated and different from the people with whom she mixed before. Also, she has no one with whom to share the small happenings of the day, things the children say and do. She has no one to make her cry, but neither has she anyone to make her laugh, except the children, and she does not often find them funny nowadays. Eating and cooking are a bore, so she does not bother unless the children are there. If she watches telvision or reads the paper, she has no one with whom to exchange ideas. She has no other adult but herself to consider, and she begins to feel shrunk, stagnant, sterile. She rates herself pathetically low, and begins to see no point of view but her own. Not unnaturally it is a cynical one; she looks confidently for snags in every situation and always seems to find them. Sometimes she makes them for herself. She is facing the very real danger of becoming totally self-absorbed.

Let us say at once that in these circumstances it is almost impossible *not* to become totally self-absorbed. But this need not last for ever. Mrs B will find that if she can accept the changes she is forced to make, and discipline herself in small ways – over meals and baths and the time she goes to bed – she will feel physically more fit and better able to make other decisions and choices. If, gradually and with help, she can put her affairs in order, she will have some spare time and attention for things and people outside herself and her home.

Mr B will need to think and to plan in very much the same way. His health will suffer if he goes on drinking and smoking at his present rate. He will need to take stock of the way he uses his spare time, and work out how he can achieve a happy relationship with his children in the limited hours he now has with them. He need not slip from aloneness into isolation, from isolation to despair. If he can think out the next twenty-year phase of his life, if he finds ways in which he can help himself, then it is quite possible for him to construct a new pattern of living.

There are ways of making life more bearable. We discuss some emergency steps that can be taken, describe rules and regulations about housing, and deal with the functions of the various social services. We explain the law in simple terms, and there is a chapter on managing money. We also talk about emotional and sexual problems and show ways in which other people have managed gradually to regain confidence, console the children, cope with loneliness and with sexual stress.

One difficulty in writing about divorce and separation is that we cannot answer your direct questions, nor can we write so fully that we touch on every problem or offer every possible answer. We attempt to deal with this difficulty in two ways: in the first place, we indicate where and from whom specific help can usually be found; secondly, we give at the end of the book a list of other publications which will provide further help and information.

You may be reading this book because you are divorced or separated, or are concerned about this possibility. On the other hand, you may have a friend or relative whose marriage has broken down. Many people in this situation wonder what they can do to help; our feeling is that it is best to give all possible *practical* help, based on the suggestions and information that we give in the following chapters. So far as the problems of the marriage itself are concerned, our advice is to leave these alone unless you are actually asked to discuss them, especially if you know both partners well.

Separation and divorce are inevitably distressing and unpleasant. No one can alter that fact. In spite of this, it is our experience that many men and women have been able to evolve and enjoy a new life, establish secure relationships for themselves and a sound future for their children.

CHAPTER 2

Law, the Lawyers and Legal Aid

The Law

THE law of divorce has developed in this country over many years. Originally, it was the Church Courts that dealt with all matrimonial cases, and the only way to get a divorce was by Act of Parliament. Naturally, this was an extremely expensive and long-drawn-out business. During Victorian times, the first changes were made in the old law, and it was at first possible for a husband to divorce his wife for adultery. Only later was she allowed to divorce him for the same reason. By 1937, the law had become much abused, and Mr Alan Herbert (the late Sir Alan Herbert) introduced a Bill into Parliament which tried to make matters more fair and realistic. This Bill became an Act, and maintained the concept of the 'matrimonial offence'. Divorces could be obtained by one spouse going to the Court and accusing the other of having 'committed' such an offence.

Although there were several changes in the law after 1937, the concept of the matrimonial offence remained until the Divorce Reform Act 1969 was passed into law. Under this Act the matrimonial offence ceased to be the basis of divorce, and instead the courts were given the power to grant divorces on the sole ground that the marriage had irretrievably broken down.

There are, under the new Divorce Reform Act, five ways of showing that a marriage has in fact broken down irretrievably:

(1) That the respondent (that is, the person who is not bringing the divorce action – the spouse who does this is called the petitioner) has committed adultery, and that the petitioner finds it intolerable to live with him or her. Adultery is an act of sexual intercourse between a man and a woman, at least one of whom is married to someone else, which is a rather complicated way of describing an act that most people understand perfectly well. The new provision goes rather beyond the old law, which

said nothing about the petitioner finding the situation intolerable. Most people doubt, however, whether this change has made very much difference, although it is clear that there are likely to be fewer divorces than there used to be based solely on one act of adultery.

(2) That the respondent has behaved in such a way that the petitioner cannot reasonably be expected to live with him or her. There is a subtle difference between this 'ground' for divorce and the previous one. Under (1) it all depends on how the petitioner feels about it, whether or not he or she can tolerate living with the respondent; but under this new rule it is for the Judge to say whether or not the petitioner can reasonably be expected to put up with the respondent's behaviour. Judges will tend to rely on what petitioners say about this, unless their reasons for wanting to live apart from their spouse are very flimsy indeed. This new rule roughly approximates to the old law relating to cruelty, which used to be one of the main matrimonial offences.

(3) That the respondent has deserted the petitioner for at least two years immediately before the presentation of the divorce petition. Under the old law the period was three years. Desertion is only valid for this purpose if it takes place without good cause. At one time under the old law, if a husband and wife tried to 'make it up' by trying a period of living together again, this cancelled out the desertion. This rule had the effect of making quite a lot of people unwilling to try a reconciliation for fear of losing their rights to a divorce. It is now possible, however, for a reconciliation period as long as six months to be tried without the petitioner losing his or her rights.

(4) That the parties have lived apart for at least two years immediately before the presentation of the petition, and the respondent does not object to the grant of a divorce. This is a completely new provision, and has by some people been called 'divorce by consent'. It really means that a couple can get a divorce by mutual agreement after they have lived apart for at least two years. Many divorces have already been granted on this basis since the Act came into effect.

(5) That the parties have lived apart for at least five years

immediately before the presentation of the petition. This was probably the most controversial of the Act's provisions for it enables the person who under the old law would have been known as 'the guilty party' to take proceedings for divorce.

These are by no means the only provisions made in the new Act; there are clauses which are designed to encourage reconciliation, which include a power given to the Judge to adjourn the proceedings once so that the possibility of reconciliation can be explored. Also, solicitors will have to discuss with their clients the possibility of reconciliation, and give them the addresses of the nearest conciliation agencies. Only time will show whether these requirements will prove effective.

The Divorce Reform Act also enables a Judge to tell the petitioner (usually, in these circumstances, the husband) that he must make fair financial provision for his wife before a divorce is finally confirmed by what is known as the Decree Absolute. Under the Matrimonial Proceedings and Property Act 1970, passed in rather a hurry by Parliament before the Divorce Reform Act 1969 came into effect, there are new provisions about the division of property between spouses, and about maintenance payments. The Courts now have the power to decide how property shall be divided between husband and wife, and can actually direct one of them to transfer it to the other. For instance, a man can be ordered to transfer his share of the matrimonial home to his wife as part of the divorce arrangement. The Judge can also order lump-sum payments by one spouse to the other, and can make directions for periodical payments to be made for the maintenance of the wife and children.

The 1970 Act says that the Judge, in deciding what order to make, must try to place the parties, 'so far as it is practicable and, having regard to their conduct, just to do so, in the financial position in which they would have been if the marriage had not broken down and each had properly discharged his or her financial obligations and responsibilities towards the other'. One effect of the two new Acts has been to place great emphasis on attempts by the parties to reach agreement with one another on the division of property and on periodical payments. There are already signs that some people are using the provisions of the new Acts to delay an agreement by holding out for better terms. This usually works only when their partner is particularly keen to get a divorce so as to marry again.

As we have already said, legal advice is essential to enable you to know how you stand under the new law. In spite of the recent changes the law is and will remain complex, for what Parliament is trying to do is to provide a set of rules that are intended to meet the emotional problems of men and women. As these problems are infinitely varied, the rules will always and inevitably fall short of perfection.

You may be worried about publicity of your divorce case, locally or in the national press. It is not likely that there will be very much of this, because over 50,000 divorces are granted each year, and only a very few attract any kind of notice. Anyone can attend the Divorce Court, which is one reason why quite a lot of people prefer to have their cases heard in the Courts in London, some way away from home and relatively anonymous. This can sometimes be arranged. The press can only report what the Judge says, not the evidence given by witnesses. This means that normally they only give the facts of the case, as stated by the Judge, and these may include a reference to the fact that the Judge 'exercised his discretion in respect of the petitioner's adultery'. Therefore, although you cannot totally avoid any publicity, the chances are that it will be small in extent. Proceedings in the Matrimonial Court, which take place before magistrates, to which we will refer later, are held privately, and the press cannot attend them.

The Lawyers

We now turn to the lawyers, men and women trained to understand the law, and to interpret its provisions as they apply to their clients. Although it is possible to obtain a law degree at a university, those who call themselves lawyers in the full sense are known as barristers and solicitors. Judges are barristers of several years' standing who have been 'elevated' to the Bench, and of course the Judges who sit and try cases in the Divorce Division of the High Court of Justice have considerable experience as practitioners in the law.

Judges are trusted – so much so, indeed, that quite frequently if people feel that a wrong judgement has been given, they seek to explain it with the rather unlikely theory that the Court has been 'deceived' by a witness. And this *is* unlikely. Lawyers see many kinds of witnesses, among them those who lie or who persistently slant the truth to their own advantage. By the time a barrister has become a Judge he has been made shrewd by experience, not least that of having in the past had to try to win cases for people whose unreliability made his task well-nigh impossible.

Judges, however, are not infallible. They do occasionally make mistakes, and the Court of Appeal exists so that these may be corrected. Nevertheless, very few matrimonial cases go to the Court of Appeal, and this is not only because of the cost involved. In addition to the professional skill which a Judge brings to a case, he may also use what is known as his discretion, and in divorce cases this is a vital factor. Whether or not a man or a woman has committed adultery is a simple question of fact, but whether a mother or father shall have custody of a child is a question of opinion – the Judge's finally. Facts help to form it, of course, but so do feelings – impressions about the two parents and their behaviour. And because Judges are human their own personalities must inevitably be to some extent reflected in the assessment which they make of the whole situation.

Many matters are within the discretion of the Judge. These include the precise amount of maintenance that a husband has to pay his wife, the frequency of access that he will be allowed if care and control of the child has been given to the mother, the grant of a divorce when a petitioner admits that he has committed adultery, and the decision as to who shall pay the costs of preparing the case and bringing it to trial. On all these points the Judge's power to use his discretion helps him to reach a fair decision about the future of the parties.

The barrister will usually need more information about the case than the Judge. He acquires this in the early stages when the action is being prepared for trial. It is the barrister's job to prepare the documents that have to be filed in the case and which the Judge sees. He does this on the basis of the 'instructions' he receives from the solicitor who has chosen him to act. The barrister will have the facts of the case in his head when it is heard, having looked carefully through the papers before coming to the Court. He will usually have a few words with his client before the case is 'called', mostly to reassure him, but also to make certain that the client knows the procedure. In fact, the hearing is not a very complicated affair. It lasts perhaps half-an-hour or even less and, although it may be a moment of great stress to the man or woman involved, you can see, by just visiting the Divorce Courts, that cases proceed one by one in a businesslike way and with little or no fuss. After all, the lawyers are handling these cases every day of their working lives, and one could not expect them to become so emotionally involved in the result as the people they are representing.

When the case is due to be heard in the Court, the Clerk reads out your name, and your barrister will ask you to go to the witness box. He may do this after explaining to the Judge the reason why the case is being brought. You have to swear that the evidence you are going to give is true, and the Clerk helps you to do this. If you are of Jewish belief or have no religious faith, then you can take the oath in a different way, but most people swear the oath by holding a copy of the New Testament in their right hand and repeating the words that are printed on a card in front of them. Next, your barrister will ask you simple questions designed to show that you have a legal right to a divorce. He may ask you to leave the witness box, and there may be one or more witnesses. The Judge may want to ask questions too; when he is satisfied he will 'pronounce judgement' and the case is over, almost before you know what is happening. It is quite normal for a barrister to be appearing for several petitioners in cases on the same day, so there is no need to be surprised if he stays in Court at the end of the case and does not leave with the client for whom he has just been acting. The solicitor will usually leave the Court with his client, and will explain the practical consequences of the Judge's decision. The great majority of cases are undefended, which means that the person who has brought the case to Court is not being opposed by his or her spouse. This enables the case to be heard quickly and means that only the petitioner need be present in Court. The petitioner's feelings are probably spared, although the speed and efficiency with which everything happens may leave him wondering whether he has been through a judicial trial or a marriage disposal unit.

The Judge does not normally decide all the issues raised in the divorce case on the day of the trial. He pronounces the Decree Nisi, later to be confirmed by the Decree Absolute making the divorce final, but he may well leave some matters to be settled 'in chambers'. This means that this part of the case will not be heard in open Court, but dealt with quite privately in another and smaller room at the Courthouse, maybe some weeks or months later. This procedure is used for decisions about custody, access to children, and the amount of maintenance that is to be paid. It is also used for applications to vary the amount of maintenance, or the provisions relating to custody or access. You are of course still entitled to be legally represented at these hearings in chambers, and they can take place without your having to attend at all, especially if the terms have been agreed in advance between you and your spouse. If you are dissatisfied with the decision, which may be made by a Registrar, who is junior to the Judge, then the case may be adjourned and a final decision reached in the Court by the Judge.

Of all the lawyers concerned, it is of course the solicitor who is most familiar with his client's problems, who sees the client several times, and who handles the case from start to finish. If someone wants legal advice, or has decided to take legal action, they go to a solicitor as a first step. If they already know a solicitor, this is fairly simple. If not, then often a friend will be able to recommend one. When the solicitor you know does not himself do much matrimonial work, he will introduce you to one of his partners who has this type of experience. You may also be able to choose a woman solicitor if you prefer. If you know no local solicitors, you can get the names and addresses of the firms in your area through the local Law Society or from the Citizens'

Advice Bureau. You then make an appointment to see the solicitor, who will take you through the story of what has happened in your marriage. You will probably find this unpleasant, for at a time of such stress you do not even want to think about, let alone discuss or describe, the things that have hurt so much over the past months and years. It cannot be helped, though, for if you are to get your legal rights it really is essential for you to tell the solicitor everything. Probably you will be taken aback at the matter-of-fact way in which he deals with it, just as if he were a doctor taking down details of your medical history. In fact, there is a similarity; both are professional men whose work demands a certain objectivity. You may find that this helps you to think and to see things more clearly, in a way that worrying about them on your own, or even discussing them with a sympathetic friend, does not. Moreover, just as most doctors do not advocate instant surgery without trying less drastic treatment, so most solicitors, before they launch divorce proceedings, will discuss at some length with their clients whether there is any prospect of reconciliation.

On the other hand, some people have told us that their solicitors have either not mentioned reconciliation or, having mentioned it, have brushed it aside and urged them on towards divorce proceedings. Whatever the approach of your particular solicitor, reconciliation is an alternative solution to your problem. You may already have considered it. In asking you to do so, your solicitor is not trying to tell you what you ought or ought not to do. It is hardly surprising that a distraught man or woman approaching a solicitor about a divorce that he or she only half wants sometimes does so in the hope that this specialist in divorce matters will say what *ought* to be done. There is the feeling that part of the responsibility for making the final decision will somehow devolve on the solicitor. This cannot be. His job is to listen to your story and to tell you your legal position, to learn from you what you want and advise you how you may legally set about achieving it. The operative word here is 'legally'. A solicitor, in telling you of the courses of action that are available to you, may suggest something which, though perfectly legal, strikes you as being morally wrong. For instance, one solicitor suggested to an ex-wife who was having difficulty in getting adequate maintenance from her former husband that she might restrict access to the children unless their father altered his attitude about the money. This action would not have been illegal; it might have worked, and if she disliked the idea all she needed to do was to reject it. Instead, she became convinced that the solicitor was a blackmailer at heart, and went off to find another. Nevertheless, the solicitor would have failed in his duty to her had he not mentioned a possible course of action which another client might have been prepared to pursue.

There may be many reasons why you do not like the advice your solicitor gives you. He may advise that you have no legal grounds for seeking a divorce, that you will not be able to succeed in a claim for custody of your child, or that you will probably have to pay more (or get less) maintenance than you expected. And, of course, he may have to tell you of the consequences of a law that you think is unfair or out-of-date, and which makes matters more difficult for you. These things often happen and it is sometimes because of them that clients blame their solicitors for the difficulties and delays that arise. Solicitors can make mistakes, but they are right far more often than not, because they know the law and they have a good deal of experience as well. So if you are involved in legal proceedings, try to contain your very understandable feelings and frustrations about what is happening to you, and pause before accusing the solicitor of handling your case badly. Changing solicitors is not to be recommended except for some very special reason. Time and, of course, money have to be spent going over the same ground a second time, and clients who change solicitors frequently are apt to get a bad name.

One way of ensuring a good working basis with your solicitor is to make sure that you tell him frankly *all* the facts of your situation, and answer carefully the questions he puts to you. To act effectively he needs your help just as much as you need his. Often it can be useful for him to have a written diary from you, telling the story of what has happened in your marriage.

So far as your case goes, your interests are your solicitor's sole concern. Whether his advice has been optimistic or pessimistic, it is still his duty to press for what you want with all his skill. If your spouse has also instructed a solicitor to act for him or her, then he too will be doing his best to get the result his client wants. Unfortunately, the average man or woman who is used to dealing with personal matters on a personal level finds it almost impossible to see their problems being fought out in legal terms without extending the battle to all sorts of side-issues. The very fact that there are two sets of lawyers, that his solicitor says, 'Well, we'll wait to see what the other side does about that,' acts as a battle cry on a client whose feelings are already inflamed. War appears to be in the air, and in no time at all it can be waged indiscriminately and in bitter earnest. Soon the solicitors are exchanging letters not only about children and maintenance, but about who gave the tea-knives and which of you owns the dog.

Although these are not uncommon or even unlikely terms for people to reach who are in the throes of divorce, they contrast sharply with the relationship that exists between the lawyers themselves. Clients are often surprised to see at some stage, possibly at the Court itself, that their lawyers, who have been arguing their case with some force, appear to be the best of friends. They probably are. The legal profession is one of the most friendly in the world, and in fact this simply has to be so. A solicitor could not possibly work effectively if he had to be personally distant or even offensive to other lawyers simply because he is handling a case in which they are opposed to one another. Next day they may be meeting at a Law Society function or corresponding in a friendly way about some ordinary matter, even cooperating on behalf of two other clients who both have a grievance against the local Council. So do not worry lest the friendliness of the lawyers means that your rights are not being protected, or that the case has been fixed. It has not.

Both barristers and solicitors have had several years of training, and practical experience, before you meet them. A barrister takes a series of examinations, works in 'chambers' where more senior barristers also practise, and learns from them. He attends lectures, reads very extensively and really earns his qualifications when he is 'called to the Bar'. Solicitors start as articled clerks, usually spending five years or more with a firm, steadily learning the job in a practical way. At the same time they take examinations which allow them very little leisure time during the last years of their period of study. This is as it should be. You have every right to expect a high degree of skill from the man or woman whom you have asked to handle your case and whose fee you will be paying.

Legal Aid

This brings us to the whole question of payment for legal advice and action, and to the availability of Legal Aid and Legal Advice. Your entitlement to Legal Aid depends essentially on your 'means', that is on the property you own, and on your income. You can get Legal Aid free if your means are small. You may have to make some contribution towards the cost if your means are moderate. What do 'small' and 'moderate' mean? To go to the bottom end of the scale, anyone receiving a supplementary benefit from the Department of Health and Social Security because their income is low, and who has not more than £125 capital, will get Legal Advice free of charge. Legal Aid, which is really action taken on your behalf for a claim you have made or for proceedings you need to take in the Courts, is available on similar terms. The cost to you depends on what is known as 'disposable income' and 'disposable capital'.

You are entitled to legal advice from a solicitor under what is known as the 'voluntary scheme', for a fee of not more than £2 for half-an-hour. If you have very little money, this charge can be as low as 12½p. The solicitor's advice will of course be brief and confined to the most simple issues, but on the basis of a short statement of your story he will be able to tell you your legal rights, and will give some idea of the amount of any contribution you may have to make under the Legal Aid and Advice Scheme.

If you are not yet ready to see a solicitor, you can visit the Citizens' Advice Bureau and ask for their help. They can give you a copy of a free leaflet called *Legal Aid and Advice – How to obtain the help of a Lawyer,* which gives full details of the way in which the Scheme works. The Citizens' Advice Bureau have considerable experience in this field, and will also be able to give you the right forms on which you can make your claim for Legal Aid, if this is what you decide to do. The free leaflet can also be obtained from the local County Court Office or from the local Legal Aid Office, whose address will be in the telephone book.

Now the application for Legal Aid will go to the local offices of the Law Society, and it has to show that you have good grounds for claiming aid. This must of course be so, because you are applying for public money to be spent on your behalf. In fact, millions of pounds each year are spent on fees to solicitors and barristers for their work for clients under the scheme. You must also give details of what you earn, of any maintenance payments you receive or make, and of your other income and your liabilities. Also you have to make a statement of what cash, property and investments you own, so that the contributions may be assessed. The leaflet we have mentioned above gives more details of this aspect of the scheme, and we do recommend you to get hold of it.

If your application for Legal Aid is approved then you will be offered a document called a 'Civil Aid Certificate', setting out the terms on which Aid will be given. The amount of your contribution will be shown, and you should obviously read the offer extremely carefully, getting help from someone else if you feel you need it. You can drop the whole thing at this stage if you like but, if you go ahead, you do so in the knowledge of what will be involved. Payments, if any, have to be made to the London office of the Legal Aid Accounts Department. You will of course be told of the various addresses to which forms are returned and money is sent, but these are also given in the leaflet that we have already mentioned.

In case of real emergency you can get immediate help from a solicitor or from the local secretary of the Legal Aid committee. It is never wise to assume that you will automatically get Legal Aid, so you should make sure about this before acting on the assumption that it is going to be available. You should not involve yourself in the expense of legal proceedings before you know that Aid will be given, unless of course you know what it will cost you and that you can afford it.

It comes as a surprise to some people that if you are awarded 'costs' by the Court, these will not necessarily be paid to you. If a woman, for instance, is awarded costs against her husband when the case is decided and he pays the greater part of the legal bills, then most or all of this will go to the Legal Aid funds and not to her. What she will get will depend on the amount of her own contributions. Another factor that surprises people is that the amount of maintenance paid to a woman under a Court order may cause her to have to pay a larger contribution to the Legal Aid fund. Conversely, the same order may have the effect of reducing the contribution that her husband, if he is also getting Legal Aid, is obliged to make towards the Legal Aid fund. If you are in doubt about this, then get advice at the beginning from the solicitor you are instructing. Do not leave everything to chance. Quite apart from anything else, it is always worrying when you do not know the amount of any bill that is coming in, so it is well worth your while making sure about this.

Magistrates' Courts

Now you may already know that it is by no means only the Divorce Courts that try cases relating to marriage problems. The magistrates (Justices of the Peace) also have wide powers to deal with matrimonial matters. They can make orders regarding:

(a) The amount of maintenance that a husband must pay his wife (or, in exceptional circumstances, a similar payment to the husband by the wife).

(b) The amount of maintenance that the husband must pay in respect of any children of the marriage.

(c) Non-cohabitation. In effect, this relieves one party from his or her normal legal obligation to live with the other. A non-cohabitation clause is put into the matrimonial order by the magistrates only if it is applied for, and even then they have a discretion whether or not to grant it. There are some circumstances in which it can even be a disadvantage to a wife to have this clause put into the order, so she should most certainly seek legal advice before asking for it.

(d) Custody of the children. This means the legal control over the children. The person to whom custody is given is their legal guardian. It is not the same thing as 'care and control'. In fact, sometimes husbands and wives agree that the wife shall have the care and control of a child while the husband remains the legal guardian. Again, both husband and wife should get legal advice before making a request to the magistrates for custody for care and control.

(e) Access to the children. It is normal for the parent who does not have the care and control of the children to be allowed to see them regularly and, in some cases, to have them away from home for a short or longer time to stay with him or her. The actual order the magistrates will make depends on all the circumstances of the case.

(f) Costs. The magistrates decide who is to pay the costs involved in bringing and defending the legal proceedings. This is a matter on which they exercise their discretion.

There are many grounds on which actions may be brought in the Magistrates' Court. The most common are the neglect of one partner (usually, of course, the husband) to maintain his spouse, adultery by one or other of the spouses, and persistent cruelty by one against the other. These are by no means the only grounds, and others include neglect to maintain children, assaults and sexual offences. If you have any doubt about whether you are entitled to take proceedings, or whether you have a good case for defending them, get legal advice as soon as possible.

How much maintenance is usually paid? What does the Court take into account when deciding about custody and access? Why is it sometimes unwise to have a non-cohabitation clause put in a matrimonial order? Well, briefly the amount of maintenance in the Divorce Courts and the Magistrates' Courts awarded to a wife is often one-third of the joint income of husband and wife; this applies with less force when the income of the husband is low, in which case he may find himself paying a good deal more than his proportion of his income to his wife. Also, we do stress that the figure of one-third is not a legally binding rule, and it may well be that a husband will be ordered to pay more or less than this. When considering what order to make about the custody of a child, the Court takes into account the facilities available for the care of the child, the accommodation available and the suitability of the parents. To give an example, a husband might be felt by far the most suitable parent to have both custody and care and control of his small son, and be able to provide good accommodation. But if he is not able to show that there will be someone to look after the boy while he is away at work, then care and control may after all be given to his wife. In these circumstances he would probably be given custody. Children are never awarded to the 'innocent' party purely as a 'reward' for good behaviour. The court considers only the interests of the child, and the behaviour of the parents is relevant only in so far as it affects this. It can be unwise for a wife to ask for a non-cohabitation clause in a matrimonial order if she may later want to divorce her husband on the grounds that he has deserted her.

Not only are the answers in the above paragraph brief, but they by no means cover all the problems of maintenance, custody and desertion. In all these matters, and indeed in any problem relating to legal proceedings, we do urge that before taking action that you cannot go back on, you should first get legal advice. Nevertheless, you are not forced to employ a lawyer, and on some occasions it is best to go straight to the Magistrates' Clerk who will help you make the application for yourself. This can be the best course when it is just a simple matter of asking for an order for maintenance, or applying for an existing order to be altered.

We have already mentioned the attitude of the Courts to the custody of children. Magistrates' Courts do have the power, if they think it right, to ask the Local Authority to take the children into its care for whatever may be an appropriate period, and for this purpose they may call on the help of the Child Care Officer who is attached to the Court. Another Court official is the Probation Officer who, in spite of the fact that his (or her) prime duty is to look after criminal offenders, can often be involved in a lot of reconciliation work. Probation Officers are handling over 40,000 'matrimonial' cases a year, and well over half of these involve some attempt at reconciliation. The magistrates may sometimes invite the parties to seek help from the Probation Officer in resolving their difficulty.

All Courts are in fact very much interested in the possibility of a reconciliation. They may sometimes adjourn a case for some days or weeks so as to give the husband and wife a chance to settle their differences, or at least to reach agreement on some of the points at issue. Besides Probation Officers, there are the Marriage Guidance Councils, clergymen and of course the lawyers themselves, many of whom are willing to make strong efforts to bring about a reconciliation, or at least to narrow the area of disagreement. It quite often happens that, even if a Court does make a matrimonial order or a decree of divorce, the lawyers or others may have helped the parties to reach agreement on some issues. This can only be a good thing, for it reduces not only the costs of the action but also the amount of distress and quarrelling, and even the effect on the children and on the husband and wife themselves.

If agreement is not possible, the County Courts and the High Court do have the power to make orders about the division of property. For instance, if a house was bought partly with a legacy the wife received, but the husband has made all the mortgage payments; if some of the furniture is hers and some his, and some bought with money given to them both as a wedding present, then the Court has the power to decide what property, and in what proportion, belongs to each of them. This decision is again very complicated, and if at all possible it is best to reach agreement, but you should do this with the benefit of legal advice.

Feelings and the Law

We have said a lot about the law and the lawyers, about the rules and the orders that can be made. But what about you and your feelings? It is one thing to be entitled to a matrimonial order, to a divorce, to custody – but you may not really *want* any of these things. Mrs C went to her solicitor:

'I want a divorce,' she said. 'He has committed adultery with some woman he met while away from home at a training course, told me about it some time after he got back, and I am going to teach him that he can't treat me like that.'

The solicitor looked into the case, and quite clearly Mrs C was entitled to a divorce if she really wanted one. She would also in all probability be given custody of the two children, because Courts usually award custody of small children to the mother. She would certainly be given an order for maintenance for herself and for them, and there was a lot of property to which she had a valid claim. But in fact her solicitor, who knew Mrs C and her husband fairly well, did not go straight off to put the legal wheels in motion. He took down her statement carefully, so that he could advise her and also take action on her behalf if this was what she really wanted, but when she had finished he told her that he needed to consider the position and would see her again in ten days' time. In fact, when she got home she felt a good deal better because for the first time she had been able to get the whole story off her chest. She liked the way her solicitor had listened to her without taking sides, and she was a little surprised to find that she felt less badly about the whole thing. A few days later she got a sad little note from her husband, who had gone away when she asked him to, wanting to know about the children, and, by the time the next appointment with the solicitor came round, Mrs C told him to put off taking any legal steps – for the time being.

Mrs C's story is not intended to prove a moral. It is only an illustration of the fact that while you are entitled to enforce your legal rights you may not wish to do so. Or you may want to postpone a decision and see how things turn out. But whatever you decide, try to do it in the knowledge of what you feel and what you want, and not just as a means of revenge. Revenge is not sweet; punishment can leave you with a very bitter taste. More satisfactory is to work out the pros and cons of taking legal action. Ask yourself what you really *want* to happen, and then see how the action you are thinking of taking relates to this.

Mr D's wife deserted him. She went off about four months after they married, returning to live with her mother and father. After his first distress and shock he became resentful, and many of his friends told him that he should not put up with this kind of conduct, that she was the one who was in the wrong, that the best thing to do was to cut his losses, find a better woman and start divorce proceedings as soon as he legally could. He got advice from a solicitor, who said that legally he certainly could do this. A little later he was talking to his grandmother, who didn't try to interfere but asked him what he really wanted to happen now, and he found himself saying that he really wanted most of all to start again with Mrs D, because he was still very fond of her and thought that perhaps he had something to do with her going away. He made contact with Mrs D, and found that she wasn't really enjoying life with mother. Oddly enough, the more her mother blamed Mr D for what had happened, the more Mrs D found herself taking his side. They decided to try again and to move to another town. This would never have happened if Mr D had acted on his full legal rights.

Once again, we are not trying to point morals. If Mr D had decided that the relationship was dead, that he would never make it up with his wife and that divorce was the only answer, then he could have gone ahead and in due time have started life again with someone else. But this would have been a decision made in the knowledge of what he really wanted, and not just on the basis of bitter feelings and resentment.

Wills and Guardianship

Finally, we want to add a few words about some other legal consequences of separation and divorce. Have you made a Will, and in it have you appointed a Guardian for your children? The appointment of a Guardian is not a simple matter, and legal advice is essential. Suppose that Mrs E, who divorced her husband three years ago, wants to appoint her sister as Guardian of her two children if she should die. This can be done in her

Will, provided it is drawn up by a lawyer, but of course it is always possible that Mrs E's husband may have objections when the time comes. If the children are still under age at the date of Mrs E's death, her husband could always apply to the Court for custody, and the Judge would certainly take his claim very seriously. This is an aspect on which Mrs E must get legal advice, and it could even be wise to make contact with her former husband about it. Another person who must of course be consulted is Mrs E's sister; she should be asked whether this is a responsibility that she is willing to take on, for however much she likes the children she might not be able to face the prospect of taking them into her home.

Wills are most often used to dispose of property. You may have some money to give away, jewellery to bequeath; you may want some of your family to receive a higher proportion of your property than others. The law is that if you make no Will your property is distributed among your near relatives according to a complicated set of rules. It may very well be that these rules do not suit your wishes at all, in which case a Will is essential. It is always best to make a Will long before you think it remotely necessary. It is surprising how many people do not make Wills, because they are superstitious about it, fearing that they may die soon afterwards. What happens if you die without leaving a Will is that your property may go to the wrong people, and that the cost of dealing with it will probably be more than it would have been if you had made the Will at a much earlier stage.

A man needs to know that there are laws which prevent him from making no reasonable provision for his dependent relatives. If his wife and children are still depending on him for the means to live, then he cannot omit them from the terms of his Will. His solicitor will advise him about this. Similarly, if a man dies and his wife feels that he has not made enough provision for her in his Will, she should get legal advice.

You have probably seen Will forms on sale in stores and in stationers' shops, and some people use these. There is no law that forces you to go to a solicitor to make your Will. At the same time, you have to be very careful when preparing a Will to use exactly the right words and to be very precise, otherwise it may later be found that a legal court-case has to be taken to discover what you meant. A good illustration of this was the man who wrote on one of these Will forms the words 'All to Mother', and signed it correctly in the presence of two witnesses. It was later discovered that he always referred to his wife as 'Mother', as did all the rest of the family. In fact his own mother was still alive, and she claimed that the property should go to her. If he had been to a solicitor in the first place, none of this trouble could have occurred. Another problem relates to the appointment of an executor. You can appoint a close relative to take on this job, provided you first ask him or her about it. Your solicitor will also be your executor if you ask him, but will charge a fee for doing so, payable when the work has to be done and not when the Will is made. Banks are also willing to act as executors of Wills, and also charge a fee.

Among the books mentioned on pp. 193–6 are some dealing with legal matters, and if you are interested in these you can buy them, or borrow them from your local library. These books, and indeed the others at your library, will give you a more comprehensive account of the law than we have done, but even then you will almost certainly need advice from a lawyer if any kind of legal action is to be taken.

CHAPTER 3

Money

MONEY is often the symbol on which we focus our anxieties, our resentments and hopes. Some people spend money to comfort themselves, and get deep into debt; others hoard it for the same reason. Between divorced and separated persons money is apt to acquire strong emotional significance both as a weapon and as a palliative. On a practical level it is often also a source of permanent, almost petrifying, anxiety.

Mr and Mrs F separated shortly after Christmas. The rows which had simmered for a year and more came to a head while Mr F stayed at home for a week, and by the New Year they had both reached the stage where they felt that separation was the only thing that could keep them sane. Mrs F decided to go, leaving their flat, taking the two children with her, and went to stay with her sister who lived in and ran a boarding house in a seaside town. She might have stayed at the flat, and this would have been wiser from many points of view, but she couldn't face her husband's anger and violence any more, and she was afraid that before long he might harm one of the children. For some time after the separation things worked fairly well for them both. They felt free, and as each blamed the other for what had happened they were both relieved to be living apart. He went on sending her the money that he had normally given her for housekeeping, less the rent of the flat and something to cover his own food. She didn't complain at the amount, partly because it was enough to cover weekly expenses, partly because she wanted to have no dealings with him.

Money only began to be a real problem after Easter, when Mrs F's sister said that she really needed all the rooms at the boarding house, unless of course Mrs F could make good the financial loss that would be involved in leaving the rooms unlet for the spring and summer. Only one of the children was at school, so Mrs F found it difficult to get any kind of job, and eventually had to write to Mr F and ask him for more money. Frankly, he thought that he was already giving her more than enough, so he didn't answer her letter. The next he heard was that she had applied to the Matrimonial Court for maintenance, and she was later awarded more than he had been paying her. He began to make the payments, though not very regularly, and even these were not enough for Mrs F to be able to stay on at her sister's house. She moved, with the children, to some smaller rooms in a much less pleasant part of the town, and still found that she had not enough money, especially on the days when Mr F failed to pay all or part of the sum the Court had ordered.

Mrs F soon had to go to the Department of Health and Social Security to apply for supplementary benefit payments, and sold her remaining jewellery to pay essential bills. Every day brought worry over money, and she found that she was getting worse and worse tempered with the children, partly because she was not eating properly. Her husband was no better off; paying the higher maintenance allowance meant first that he had to give up cigarettes, then sell his car. He was having trouble paying the rent of the flat, and he had no money for going out in the evenings. For both of them money was a constant anxiety.

This story could be repeated a hundred times, and there are many people who have had to cope with much worse situations than this one. There is no easy solution, and it does not help much to suggest that they go back to live together, because this is the one thing that they are both absolutely determined not to do. We can look at their financial problems in the short term and can also consider the more distant future. In the short term, money problems very often present a real emergency. In the longer term they are just as much a problem, but are more amenable to careful planning.

Emergency

We will start with the emergency problems. You may find yourself with nothing, or practically nothing, on which to live. If this happens, then you must go straight to the local Department of Health and Social Security and ask for their emergency help. In itself this is a hard enough step for many people to take. Some of them still think of the supplementary benefits as a kind of charity which they cannot ask for. Others dread an interview with an official, and the humiliation that they think it will involve. This is where we must say two things, quite bluntly: payments from the Department are your right, as a citizen; and asking for what you need is something that must be faced, unpleasant though it is. Perhaps if you can see the payment of supplementary benefits in the same way as you think of sickness benefits or children's allowances – and this is a perfectly reasonable way to think of them – you may find it easier to apply for help. Either a husband or wife, or maybe both, will have been steadily paying for their share of insurance stamps for some years, the money being deducted from their salary, and it is this type of payment that goes towards supplementary benefits and other Government grants. There is therefore no element of charity at all in accepting the money.

We hear a lot about people with large families and fast cars 'living on National Assistance', and it is of course this kind of story that gets into the news. But in fact the great majority of supplementary benefit payments, which have taken the place of the National Assistance scheme, are made to people who really need them and who are therefore fully entitled to receive them. In fact, it has been calculated that there are quite a lot of people who do not claim the allowances to which they are entitled, and Government publicity is often directed at those who are not getting what they should, either through ignorance or through the mistaken belief that they are somehow degraded if they accept this kind of help.

What about the other worry – facing the interview with the unknown Department official behind the desk? Now this may be the first of such interviews, and as they are bound to occur from time to time the best thing is to develop a realistic attitude to them. You will notice we do not say an 'optimistic' or a 'positive' attitude – which may be quite impossible to achieve. Nevertheless, and although this sort of difficulty is hard to face, it must be done, and afterwards you will find that it was nothing like as awful as you feared it would be. In the first place, the man or woman at the Department is a person just as much as you are, with feelings, problems, an appetite, and no doubt with money worries too, though of a different kind. We are not going to pretend that they are all good-tempered, welcoming, sympathetic and generous, but nor are they all liverish, mean or punishing. They are trying to do a job as best they can, and it is sometimes hard for them to do so in circumstances when they must feel like giving more help than they are allowed to.

One way of clearing the fog of anxiety and uncertainty is to obtain the explanatory leaflets about supplementary benefits from the Department of Health and Social Security. The most useful leaflet is S1, and to it is attached a claim form. It explains who can get benefits and how much they will receive. At the time of writing (1971), if you are not in full-time work you can have your income brought up to £5.20 a week, if you are a householder; you will also be paid the amount of your rent and rates (unless these are unreasonably high) and up to £2.40 a week for a child, depending on age. It is not quite as simple as this, of course, and there are adjustments if you have some capital or income of your own; you can earn a small amount each week without its being counted; and so on. If you are in full-time work and have a child or children, then you may be able to obtain a Family Income Supplement of up to £4 a week. Details of this are given on leaflet FIS 1. If you have any doubt about your entitlement, read the leaflets or ask the officer at the Department to explain the position to you. Or if you prefer you can get similar guidance from the local Citizens' Advice Bureau.

Do not be too surprised if going out to earn gives less return than you expect. Mrs G got herself a £10-a-week job, but after fares to and from work, paying a baby-sitter, buying more expensive food which took less time to prepare, paying income tax and an increase in Legal Aid contributions she had little extra to spend. In fact, this did not matter too much, because the relief she got from doing a job far outweighed her irritation at all the new expense. And after six months she was able to take on a better position with the same employers at £14 a week.

The payment of supplementary benefits over a period of time

is usually done by the Department giving you a book of orders which you can cash at the Post Office that you find most convenient. This is exactly the same way as Old Age Pensions and Family Allowances are paid. If your need for money is really urgent, then the officer at the Department of Health and Social Security can give you some cash straightaway, and someone will visit you at home a few days after receiving your claim form. The idea of this visit is to work out what allowance you are entitled to, and it is not just a snooping operation. There must, of course, be some means of checking on the real situation of people who apply for official support of this kind, otherwise it would be all too easy for a small minority to obtain money by making false statements.

You might think that all these rules apply only to women, but it is not so. Naturally, supplementary benefits are normally paid to the wife or former wife, for she is usually looking after the children, but the scheme applies just as much to a father who is having to cope with the same situation. The Department of Health and Social Security, when it is having to make payments to a woman whose husband is not supporting her adequately, will usually bring pressure on her to apply for maintenance at the Matrimonial Court, if she has not already done so, for in this way the cost to the Government can quite properly be reduced. The amount the Court awards depends, of course, on the needs of the wife and children, the income of the husband and the other circumstances of the case. We deal with this more fully in Chapter 2, but the usual method of collection is for the husband to pay the weekly maintenance to the Magistrates' Court, where the wife collects it. It can also happen that the husband is ordered to pay the wife direct.

Enforcing the maintenance payments can be a real problem, as it was in the case of Mr and Mrs H. Local procedures tend to differ slightly, but Mrs H went to the Court to ask what she should do when Mr H first failed to pay. She was asked to attend a hearing of the case a few days later, though if she had lived in another area she would probably only have had to sign a form. In her case the Magistrates made what is known as an 'attachment of earnings' order. This meant that Mr H's employers were required to deduct the maintenance from his weekly pay and send it to the Court, and as he had a steady job this worked quite well. It was even better for him in one way, because he never saw the money and therefore was not tempted to spend it on something else, thus landing himself with large orders for payment of arrears. There are of course some men who change jobs from time to time, some deliberately and others not, and when this happens the attachment of earnings order does not automatically transfer to the new employment. Some delay is usually involved, and the wife may need the temporary help of the Department of Health and Social Security. She can transfer her right to maintenance to the Department if her husband does not make regular payments, and then they claim the money from him. In this way she can be sure of a regular income. The Department know where the husband is because of his insurance records.

There are other ways of enforcing maintenance orders, but it is in the discretion of the Justices which method they decide to use. In serious cases a husband who refuses to pay when he could well do so can be sent to prison for up to six weeks; or the magistrates can pass a 'suspended' prison sentence, which has the effect of making him pay by a certain date if he is to avoid going to prison. This is not, though, a very common way of enforcing maintenance payments, for it is hard to prove that a man's refusal to pay was deliberate.

Many people do not know that a Magistrates' order for maintenance, or for that matter a similar order of the High Court, can be altered if there are changed circumstances. If, for instance, a husband has been earning a good deal of overtime money and has quite a lot of cash coming in each week, he will be ordered to pay an appropriate amount to his wife; but if there is less overtime work, or if he becomes redundant and has to seek a job with a lower salary, then he simply will not be able to afford the payments ordered by the Magistrates, and can go back to the Court to apply for a variation of the original order. To do this he can get help from the Clerk of the Court, or of course from a solicitor. These remarks apply just as much to maintenance or, as they were once known, alimony payments ordered by the

High Court. Applications to the High Court, however, are usually for larger sums than are ordered by the Matrimonial Courts, and must be made with the help of a solicitor. We deal in much more detail with legal action in Chapter 2.

Borrowing

We have now described the most likely ways in which a man or a woman can obtain money in an emergency, but of course there are others. For some people it is possible, and wise, to borrow money to help over a critical period. Borrowing can be done in different ways: it can be a formal affair, arranged through a bank or Loan Company, or it can be a purely private and family matter. The vital thing is to be sure of being able to repay the loan as you have arranged to do. First let us look at the private loan: Mrs J and her husband drifted apart after a long period of bickering, and when he finally vanished he left no address. At a later stage she was able to trace him and get a maintenance order from the Magistrates' Court, but this didn't solve her immediate problem. The children were at school, and she found that she could get quite a good daytime job provided she had a car which she could use. The employers were not willing to give her a car, but they did make a generous mileage allowance which would enable her to run and replace one. She could probably have found some sort of vehicle for £200 or so, but everyone advised her to buy something better and more reliable which would last and would carry at least a six-month guarantee. She soon saw exactly the right car, which had been well maintained and had only had one owner. It had been continuously serviced by the local garage, whose manager she knew slightly, and would cost her £400.

The trouble was that the monthly cost of buying the car on hire-purchase was more than Mrs J could afford. Eventually, after thinking of giving up her job, she mentioned the problem to her uncle, who had told her that he would help if he could as soon as he heard of the separation. He said he was glad to lend her the money, which he took out of his own savings; he only wanted to be paid the interest that he was losing by cashing savings and suggested that she should try to pay him back over a period of three years or so. After eighteen months' work on the new job she had managed to pay just over £200 back, partly out of the mileage allowance, when her uncle died. Very fortunately they had made a note of the terms of the loan when it was first made, and therefore his executor did not have to ask Mrs J to make an immediate repayment of the loan. If there had been nothing in writing and Mrs J had admitted that she still owed £200, then the executor might have had to ask her for immediate repayment which could have resulted in her having to sell the car. As it was, she was able to pay off the final part of the loan, and all was well.

The point of Mrs J's story, of course, is that whatever arrangements you make for loans, whether they are from friends, relatives or anyone else, you really must record the terms of the agreement on a sheet of paper. Both people then keep a copy of the sheet signed by the other. There is of course more to this sort of arrangement than keeping a record of it. For instance, most people do not like asking for a loan at all, and if this is the way you feel it is best to work out the terms on which you can manage to repay *before* you make the approach to anyone for help. By saying this we do not mean that you write the terms down and present them to the person who may be able to lend you the money, but it is sensible to have in mind what you can in fact afford to make by way of repayments. When it is the man who needs money it is sometimes possible for him to ask his employer for an advance of salary, to be deducted over a period of months from his monthly or weekly wage. Of course, there are firms who are not willing to enter into this sort of arrangement, and it will be possible only when an employee is well known to his employers and has probably worked for them for quite some time.

It is also possible, of course, for some people to borrow money from a bank, but arrangements with banks come into a rather different category. Mr K had a good job when he separated from his wife. They decided that he would leave the house in which they had been living, and as he wanted to provide a decent home for his children he agreed to keep on with the mortgage payments. He might have been able to pay his wife enough money to buy food, clothes and so on, whilst he lived cheaply in rooms, but this was not the way things worked out, for he had by then met another woman whom he wanted to marry. Many practical problems arose: Mrs K was taking divorce proceedings, which were bound to cost Mr K a lot of money, for even if he did not defend the action costs would probably have been awarded against him. Yet how could he pay these and at the same time get a new house, as well as maintain the payments on the old one?

Mr K went to the bank manager, who was sympathetic but explained that he could only lend money if Mr K could offer some kind of 'security'. In other words, if Mr K were given a loan, and had difficulty repaying it, the bank wanted to be sure of getting its money back. Mr K had already mortgaged his first house, borrowing as much money as the Building Society would lend, so that was no use to him as security for the bank loan. However, he did have two life-insurance policies that had not been affected by the arrangements made with his wife concerning the divorce and, as he had been paying the premiums for over fifteen years, they were worth a certain amount of money to him. Eventually he was able to obtain a loan from the bank (of rather less than he had hoped) by depositing the insurance policies with them and signing legal documents which protected the bank's interest in them.

Another way of getting the loan would have been to find a guarantor to back it. If Mr K could have persuaded some friend or relative to guarantee the loan, and to give the bank adequate security, then he would probably have been able to borrow more money. In fact he did not do this, partly because he did not want to be under an obligation to someone else and partly because he was doubtful whether anyone would guarantee his debt. Difficult relationships often result from personal loans and guarantees, and therefore they are best avoided if there is any alternative.

Selling

Another source of cash can be one's own savings or property. Perhaps we can go back to Mrs J and her car for a moment: suppose there had been no generous uncle, would she have had to give up all idea of the job? Not necessarily. If she had some savings she could have cashed them. If she had some jewellery she could have sold it, probably for a good deal more than it originally cost. This might well have been hard for her to do, especially if the jewellery was a family piece. It would have been just as difficult to decide to sell an antique desk, the silver cutlery or a picture. But in spite of the difficulty, and the distress of having to part with something that has an emotional value as well as a cash one, it is an idea that Mrs J should consider seriously. Is it not worth while to take this one opportunity to secure herself a job now rather than hang on to the piece of jewellery or furniture that might later have to go anyway? This is not a decision that we could make for Mrs J, or for anyone else, but she should at least know that the things she owns can often be turned into cash – in an emergency.

It is one thing deciding to sell your property, but quite another to know *how* to do so. We suggest that you get advice from your bank manager, from a solicitor, or from someone else who knows reputable firms in your area dealing in the kind of goods you have to sell. If possible, get more than one offer so that you can compare them; and remember that an advertisement in the local paper can bring in quite a lot of replies. Once the item is sold, any number of people will be only too ready to tell you that you did not get enough for it, and this can add to your feelings of guilt at having to sell in the first place. The chances are that, in spite of what they say, they could not have done any better. Once the thing has been sold it has gone, and that is an end of it. Use the money as planned, and leave other people to do the worrying.

Other Benefits

The next thing you need to know about is the money benefits to which you may be entitled. Take income tax: it is quite possible for a couple who are parting to arrange matters so that a minimum amount of tax has to be paid, but this can only be done if they go about it in the right way. Income tax law is extremely complicated, and they will need an accountant's advice. The need for help tends to apply more to the man than to the woman, but it is in the interests of them both to get help at an early stage. We well know that this is easy to say but hard to achieve. The last thing that a man and a woman who are at loggerheads are likely to do is reach an agreement. But it is worth trying. From the husband's point of view, the less tax he has to pay the more he has to spend; from the wife's angle, she may find that she too will receive a higher payment if her husband is able to take advantage of legal means of reducing his tax burden. Of course, you have to pay an accountant's fee, but most people find that he saves them much more in tax than they have to pay him for his services.

It may also help you to know what happens after an agreement has been reached over maintenance payments, or after a Court has made an order. Briefly, a husband deducts tax from payments he makes under the terms of any separation agreement made with his wife, unless of course the agreement provides for him to make payments 'net' of tax. He also deducts tax from payments made under a Court order, except small payments made by the Magistrates' Court. Now the husband pays tax to the Inland Revenue, and it is up to the wife to reclaim any tax that she is not due to pay. She can do this through her solicitor, or she can apply to the Inspector of Taxes in her own district who will help her. Also, of course, she can ask help from an accountant. Magistrates' Courts send a note to the Inspector of Taxes of maintenance orders that have been made, which will mean an alteration of the tax coding of husband and wife, if they are both earning. This simple summary may give you the impression that tax matters give few problems. It is not so, but the kind of difficulties that do arise are technical and you will need skilled help with them. Get this help early rather than too late.

There are several cash benefits available for people with low incomes, many of whom may be divorced or separated. There are rent and rates rebates, which can be obtained by applying to your local Council offices. Schemes vary from area to area, so you have to ask about this and cannot rely on what someone else has told you. Relief from rates is available for people with incomes of £9 a week or less, and the limit goes up by £2 for every child of the family. Low income families can also obtain free milk, orange juice and vitamins. This is the kind of service that you *must* take advantage of, for it will not only save your pocket but also give you and your children the means to stay healthy. The Department of Health and Social Security will tell you how to get these foods free.

There are other benefits given free to people with low incomes. They can obtain clothes for their children, free, or for a small charge; they can be given grants for school uniforms, and if their children stay on at school after the age of fifteen an 'educational maintenance allowance' can be claimed. They may be able to obtain exemption from paying charges for dental treatment or for glasses, and to claim repayment of prescription charges; and they can get free school meals for the children as well. Money is also available for 'exceptional needs', such as household equipment, removal expenses and essential decorations. For most of these benefits, apply to the Department. For those relating to the school, ask the Local Education Authority, whose address is in the telephone book.

Then there is the National Insurance scheme. You may know that National Insurance benefits depend on the payments that a husband or wife have made, by stamping a card, under the scheme. If you are employed, this is done for you by your employers, and if you work for yourself you must stamp your own card. When contributions have been kept up to date then you are fully entitled to all benefits under the National Insurance scheme, but if contributions have been reduced for some reason then the payments that can be made to you are affected. The Department of Health and Social Security will give you a form,

NI27, which explains how those with small incomes can apply to be excused from paying National Insurance. Another useful form is NI95, called *Women whose marriage is ended by divorce or annulment,* which makes the point that a woman whose marriage has been ended should immediately tell the local Department of Health and Social Security. The most sensible thing is to go round there and have the whole position explained to you. Take away one of these leaflets to read and, if things are still not clear, go back and ask again. Briefly, when she is divorced, a woman can no longer rely on her husband's National Insurance payments to maintain her rights.

After reading the above paragraphs, you may still have no idea what your entitlements under the National Insurance scheme are or should be, or what it is best to do. In this case, go on asking until you *do* understand. If one office cannot make themselves clear to you, and we know this is possible, try somewhere else. We mean by this that, if you have sought advice, say, at the Citizens' Advice Bureau or at the local Council offices, and the person there did not seem to know very much about the scheme, then go to the Department of Health and Social Security. On the other hand, if the officer at the Department was not clear, by all means visit the Citizens' Advice Bureau, and someone there may telephone the Department official for you, sort the problem out and explain it to you. This is just the sort of job they are there to do. Do not leave yourself in a state of doubt or ignorance, for later these benefits under the National Insurance scheme may be very important to you.

You may feel that other people react differently to you in your new situation. Try not to be too surprised or upset about this, for it can happen by accident. You may visit some official at the end of a week when you are tired, and he has already answered the same question four times that day. If the interview should be a bad one, you will leave feeling angry, miserable or cut off. Now how can you deal with this? There are several ways, the least effective of which is to complain to the man's superior. One suggestion is to return, apologize for any misunderstanding and ask the same question again. For various good reasons we know this may be absolutely impossible; if so, you can try writing a letter to the office putting your point clearly.

Mrs L had a problem of this kind: she had been granted Legal Aid for her divorce case, and at one stage she was given an order by the Court that her ex-husband should pay her a fairly large sum of money to compensate her for some furniture and other articles he was using and which partly belonged to her. A well-meaning friend said that she would be lucky to see any of this money, as it would be taken by the Legal Aid authorities as a contribution to her solicitor's fees and expenses. She got very worried and telephoned her solicitor, who said he would make inquiries. After a delay she also went to see an officer at the Department of Health and Social Security who had made the original visit to her home when she first applied for Legal Aid, his job being to assess what her financial position then was. The second interview with him was completely unsatisfactory; he did not appear to know anything, nor did Mrs L think he was in the least interested. She was upset and rude to him. He retreated behind a haughty wall of silence. After she had left his office she collapsed into tears and felt dreadful. But she was not a girl easily put off, and two days later she wrote to the Law Society's London office of the Legal Aid scheme, explaining in three long and closely-written pages how much she needed the money for the children's clothes and new radiators. Did they have to take it all, she asked? In fact, the Law Society were not only reasonable but charming. Mrs L had a very polite letter saying that she need only make quite a small contribution out of her cash award towards the costs; in the end she was able to buy both clothes and radiators, and had some money left over.

A woman will find that she always scores by charm rather than by aggression, in fact by using her femininity. It will then be other people's pleasure to help her. Look at it this way: what kind of approach do *you* respond to? The demanding and dictatorial? The whining complaint? Or one that is friendly and frank?

Persistence, a capacity to realize and to admit that one is sometimes wrong, and acceptance that other people do behave unpleasantly from time to time, are of great value. So is a sense of humour. These qualities take time to cultivate, especially if you have not had to battle for yourself in the past. All the same, it is worth going doggedly on to get what you need. You may feel that this puts the tougher people in a better position than the rest, and we are bound to admit that you are right. But we have seen a lot of women, and men, grit their teeth and struggle for what they and their children need, and having got it found the confidence to do even better next time.

More Money Matters

There are many other money matters that may affect you, ranging from hire purchase, pensions and insurance to banks, building societies, mortgages and new savings. Our aim here is to give you some general guidelines, but if you have problems you should always get help. And help really is available, from bank managers, from solicitors, from friends, from clubs and the Social Services.

We will start with hire purchase. Some means of buying property by instalments are sensible and useful; a man who needs a car and who only has enough money to pay half its cost may be wise to buy one on hire purchase, spreading the payments – and the loan interest – over two or three years. A woman may acquire a bed and other furniture the same way. It is vital for them to be certain of two things: that they can afford the monthly payments as they fall due, and that they really do need the thing they are going to buy.

It is very easy to buy goods just to comfort yourself; just spending money can make you feel better. In addition, the job of a salesman, whether he is showing you a car or a brush, is to be friendly, to encourage and to put you in the frame of mind in which you want to buy. He may also put on other pressures, suggesting that the goods may soon be sold out or go up in price, and he will show his disapproval if it looks as if you are not going to buy. We all want to be liked, and approved of, and to be thought wise and sensible. Salesmen are aware of this, and their sales talk is often pitched accordingly. When one's spirits are low it is particularly difficult not to be influenced by what is neither more nor less than advertising technique. So do decide first whether you really need the thing you are buying, and find out its price in advance.

Then, can you afford it? You may have the money for the down payment and for the next month's instalment, but what about the following months, and what will be the effect on the rest of your budget? We have something to say about budgeting in Chapter 6. Be sure the money is going to be there when you need it. You can also investigate other methods of buying, and consider whether a better opportunity to buy may not come in a few weeks or months, e.g. when the sales open. You may decide to buy some things secondhand at a local sale or through newspaper advertisements. Interest rates are high on goods bought on hire purchase, often working out at twenty per cent or more, and it may be worth a visit to your bank to see whether you can borrow more cheaply from them, probably paying interest at eight per cent or less.

Let us go on to discuss banks. There is no law that makes you have a bank account, but it certainly can be most convenient to pay bills by cheque. Banks are always glad to have your money, to keep it for you until you need it, and as long as there is a credit balance on your account they will honour your cheques. They will also perform other services for you, like making regular monthly or yearly payments on your behalf, arranging for foreign currency to be available, and so on. They charge for these services, so it is best to check first with the bank manager what it will cost you to keep an account.

You can open rather similar accounts at the nearest Trustee Savings Bank, which is a Government agency. The atmosphere is rather like your local Council offices there, being more fussy than in the commercial banks; also, they normally expect you to have a minimum of £50 deposited with them in a savings account, which the other banks do not demand. With any bank account it goes without saying that you must keep a careful note of the cheques you have drawn, so that you know how much you have left. If you have any doubts about banking, see the bank manager; he will explain the whole procedure for opening an account, and will be glad to see you.

Nowadays you can also deposit money with the Post Office Giro, which is another kind of account, held with the Post Office, and which you can use to pay ordinary bills like those from the Gas and Electricity Boards. The Giro account charges are very low, and the system is fairly simple, but you cannot overdraw the account. Details are available at all Post Offices, where arrangements can also be made for you to withdraw money from your Giro account if you wish.

Neither the banks nor the Post Office will normally pay you interest on your money, unless you have a 'deposit account' with them. You cannot draw cheques on deposit accounts. So if you have enough cash to earn you some worthwhile interest you can put it into a Post Office deposit account, or deposit it with your bank, or with a Building Society, telling them what you want. Building Societies pay their interest free of tax, which can really be worth your while if you normally pay tax at a high rate. The higher the rate of income tax you have to pay, the better the Building Society deposit works for you. Some people who have mastered the techniques of accounting keep their money with Building Societies until they need it for regular payments. A man who has big fuel bills to meet in December, and a life insurance payment in January, can start saving regularly in the Spring, putting the money in a Building Society account each month. At the end of the year he will have some useful interest, as well as the cash to pay the bills.

You can use these deposit accounts for your savings, too, although you should also consider whether this is the best method of saving. For those in a position to put a certain amount of money aside regularly, it is well worth while thinking of investment in unit trusts. These are regularly advertised in the Sunday newspapers, and you can get advice from a bank manager, a solicitor or a stockbroker about them. The advantage of these unit trusts is that they tend to rise in value over a period of time, while the cash you have saved tends to drop in value. The managers of the unit trust invest your money, and the money paid by many other people, in the shares of public companies.

In this way your own fairly small savings take a share in a very large investment, and your risk is spread widely.

Life insurance is another way of saving regularly. There are several types of life insurance. Some life insurance policies just give a cash sum when a person dies, and nothing before then. Others give the sum on a specified date, such as the day you reach sixty years of age. The best, but of course the most expensive, policies are 'with profits'. They guarantee to pay you a minimum sum on death or retirement, whichever happens first, in the same way as the other policies, but they also grow steadily as the years go by, attracting profits which the insurance company gives you. Insurance policies of this kind can give you the assurance that your dependants will have some provision if you die young. They can be used to buy a pension when you retire, and can often help you to borrow money when you need it. In addition, you can direct the insurance company to pay the money to a particular person on your death. If you are thinking about insurance, approach an insurance company or an insurance broker for advice. If the broker is a reputable one, and most are, he will look round for the best bargain from your point of view. Just tell him what you want, and you will not have to pay him any fee. He gets his profit from the commission that the insurance company pays him. This means, of course, that he will be keen for you to take out an insurance policy so, as with goods bought on hire purchase, be sure you get the policy you need.

This advice applies just as much to other insurance, such as fire insurance or insurance against injury, theft or damage to a car. In one way, and although insurance people do not describe it like this, insurance is a kind of bet with the insurance company. We do not want to take this analogy with betting too far, naturally, for real betting and gaming is legally a very different thing from insurance. In fact, a real gaming bet should be seen as spending luxury money, if you are going to try it at all. For anyone who is at all short of cash, betting is the least advisable way to spend money. Insurance, on the other hand, can be a form of protection both from risk and anxiety. If you have an innate urge to gamble, you can indulge it by putting any spare money into Premium Bonds, which may give you tax-free prizes; every month you stand to win a large sum of money, and there is no loss of your original investment.

We mentioned Building Societies earlier, and of course you will know that they also exist to lend money as well as to borrow it. They work by accepting cash on deposit from thousands of people, and lending it back to much fewer numbers. They make their profit by the difference between the interest they charge and the interest they pay, and there are laws governing the proportion of their assets that must be in easily realizable form. If you want to buy a house on mortgage you should consult a Building Society. You will find that you have a better chance of getting their help if you already have cash deposited with them.

Mortgages can also be obtained from insurance companies, usually linked with life policies, from private individuals and from local Councils. If you need a mortgage, discuss it with the solicitor who is acting for you on the purchase of your home, and approach the Building Society, the Council or an insurance broker, depending on your need. Normally, mortgages with insurance companies only suit people paying a high rate of income tax; mortgages from local Councils are most often granted for properties of smaller value, or built many years ago.

Lastly, pensions. We have mentioned the National Insurance scheme, and it is normal for employers to deduct from wages a sum which eventually allows you to claim a 'graduated pension'. Details will be explained to you at the local Department of Health and Social Security offices, or at a Citizens' Advice Bureau. We have described life insurance policies; these can be turned into annuities, which are annual, quarterly or monthly payments made to you by the insurance company, and operate as a kind of pension. Many firms also have pension schemes, and this is quite an important factor when you are applying for a job. The time to start thinking of a pension is long before you are going to need it, for the earlier you start making contributions the more you will get when the time comes for your retirement.

Whether a divorced wife will be entitled to any part of her husband's pension given to him by his firm, and whether she will get a pension under the National Insurance scheme, will depend on the terms of the divorce in the first case, and on the contributions he has made towards a pension in the second. This is a difficult matter, and a woman should ask her solicitor's help with it when she is starting the divorce action – or when it is being brought against her – and should not leave it to chance. A man should also get legal advice about his pension rights, and the extent to which he will be expected to keep these for his former wife. This can be very important to him, expecially if he is planning to marry again, for he may find himself in the position of having to make provision for two families.

Another way you may receive money is from the estate of someone who has died, perhaps under the terms of their Will, or under the law of intestacy if they leave no Will.

We have tried to cover all the main problems and the ways in which you can get help with money problems. Do try to get help when you need it, and don't be put off too easily. There are people around who are willing and able to help, and if you persist you will find them.

CHAPTER 4

Housing

'If you are going to write about housing, it will be the most depressing chapter in your book.'

This was said with sad, quiet conviction by a worker for the Citizens' Advice Bureau with thirty years' experience of trying to help people with problems of every kind. The Bureaux receive hundreds of thousands of inquiries each year about housing, and about the rights of landlords and tenants. Their help is very necessary, for the law relating to rents, rates and property is extremely complex. It is not only the law that creates problems: on a practical level, simply finding somewhere to live can be incredibly difficult. It is hard enough for the newly-married, but it becomes even more urgent where there are children, more worrying when there is no money, and more awful when there is a background of distress and uncertainty. When people separate, a hundred questions arise. Who owns the house or the tenancy? Who has made the mortgage or the rental payments? Who wants to go on living in the home, and will he or she be able to afford to do so? What is to happen to the one that is going to move out? Who will help or advise? What are the alternatives?

At the moment of separation it is not only that two people are going to live apart and to make separate lives. If you think of all the thought, pride, planning and hard cash that have gone into the making of a home, it is not surprising that to break it up and to make out of it two new and independent units will create serious practical, financial and emotional problems. As with almost all the other problems facing the divorced or separated person, it is best to look carefully at the alternatives before you decide what to do. If the atmosphere is not too bad, it may be possible to discuss them together; if this is not possible, then it will be worth your while to discuss the alternatives with an independent person, and do think carefully before acting.

What are the alternatives? The first is to stay where you are, to continue in the matrimonial home. Needless to say this is far from simple: how is it to be decided who will leave? Usually the person who finds the situation the most intolerable will be the one to go, but what if she – or he – is going to take the children? Unless there are exceptional circumstances, lawyers and social workers will normally advise the woman to stay in the matrimonial home with the children. There are both practical and legal reasons for this. A man finds it much easier to obtain a place to live on his own, and once a wife has left the matrimonial home it becomes much harder – sometimes even impossible – to enforce any rights she may have to occupation. In addition, the disturbance to the children is usually less if they continue to live in the place that they know.

Let us look more closely at the way things happen. Many couples who are owners of their own home have had the title deeds drawn so that the place is in their joint names. At the beginning, sharing was part of the mood of the marriage. Also, if one of them should die there would be fewer legal and death duty complications. If the marriage breaks up, however, the house may have to be sold and the proceeds divided between them, unless some agreement can be reached. Other complications can arise if one partner is the legal owner but the other has made contributions towards the cost of the property or the mortgage payments, or has made some other indirect contribution which enabled them to buy or live in the house. If there are problems of this kind it is invariably wise to seek legal advice before reaching any agreement about the sale of the house, or any other binding and permanent arrangement. This normally applies more to wives than to husbands, but even if a wife has made no financial or practical contribution towards the purchase or maintenance of a house, she should still take steps to protect her legal right to stay there. This can be done by registration of her 'Wife's Right' at the Land Charges Registry. Advice about this can be obtained from a solicitor or from the Citizens' Advice Bureau.

It may not be a simple matter of agreement between husband and wife, for other parties may be involved. A husband cannot turn his wife out of the house that is in his sole name, but a Building Society, insurance company or some other mortgagee can do so if the mortgage payments are not kept up. More than one embittered husband has used this knowledge to try to revenge himself on his wife by going away and refusing to pay the mortgage instalments as they fell due. This is a sad and desperate action which very often does as much harm to him in the long run as it does to her, and most of all to the children. In such a case, or even when husband and wife have parted on fairly amicable terms, some people may take paying guests or let part of a house in order to be able to afford the mortgage payments. The trouble here is that the terms of the mortgage will almost always forbid this, and if the mortgagee (the person who has loaned the money) learns that boarders, lodgers or paying guests are being taken in, there is the risk that both the tenant *and* the owner may be turned out.

Another problem of turning landlord as a means of boosting income is that it can easily give rise to a claim for income tax. On the other hand, with an accountant's help, you may be able to set off some household expenses against this tax.

Where a couple have rented a house or flat in their joint names, the wife who has been deserted by her husband is reasonably well protected, in that she cannot be turned out of the house by him, but of course the rental payments still have to be met, also the rates on the property if these are a tenant's responsibility under the terms of the lease. We mention this problem in Chapter 5 under the heading *Getting Help* when we discuss ways in which a wife can obtain money for the rent, but there are other problems if the tenancy is in her husband's name, and it may be necessary for her to register her Wife's Right as mentioned above. This she should do before the legal dissolution of the marriage by divorce, as the Right cannot be registered if they are no longer married. The rules about this are in a recent Act of Parliament called the Matrimonial Homes Act 1967.

From what we have said it is absolutely clear that anyone who is thinking of leaving home, especially a woman with children, should first take legal advice. An action of this kind should only be taken in the knowledge of what it will involve, and although this may not alter your decision to leave, you will at least be aware of how you stand, which may make you behave rather differently.

If the decision has been made to separate and to set up different homes, one possibility, and sometimes the only one open to you, may be to live with relatives or friends, at any rate for a time. If you are able to make this sort of arrangement it will mean that you will be sharing your home with someone else. Sharing can be a pleasure and can have many advantages – or it can be utter misery. If you are sharing a home for the first time you need to know that the arrangement is most likely to succeed if you can learn to *leave each other alone*. This applies as much to strangers sharing a house as it does to a mother and daughter living in the same home. Sons often succeed in sharing more successfully than daughters, simply because they are out of the house for more of the time. Just because you are living close to someone else, do not expect to know everything about their affairs. Do not waylay your neighbours with conversation on the stairs so often that they feel they cannot come and go in their own house without first checking that the coast is clear. Do not pour out too many confidences about yourself in rash moments, or fill your duller times with speculation about what your neighbours are doing. If there are to be rules (there are bound to be some, though the fewer the better) it is best to have them stated pleasantly but firmly right from the start, and then each can respect the freedom and independence of the other without fussing over small details that do not really matter. People find that after a divorce it is sometimes particularly difficult to share with relatives, who are too concerned about what has happened. Emotions are probably running high, and unwanted advice and interference can cause a lot of resentment.

We heard of a divorced woman who, with her daughter, was offered free accommodation in her parents' home. Short of money and with nowhere to live, she gratefully accepted. Having someone to look after the child made it possible for her to take a very good, full-time job. With a high salary and no major household expenses she was able quite easily to support her daughter through school and university. This woman valued her career, and for years the advantages of the living arrangements far outweighed any small domestic restrictions. In middle age, with less interest in career prospects, and no apparent possibility of remarriage, she felt trapped, disillusioned and bitter. Her daughter married and went abroad and her parents were older and more demanding. In return for a certain kind of security she felt she had forfeited all personal freedom for the duration of her parents' lives, and missed opportunities that would never come to her again. Housing was at the root of this problem, but so too was the conflict that many divorced women feel between children, parents, career and personal independence.

One answer to the housing problem is to rent, because it may be impossible to buy a place outright. For a woman who is on her own this is usually possible, as it is for a man. Landlords – and landladies – are sometimes dubious, however, about letting to an unsupported – or partially supported – mother. There are several reasons, the most obvious of which is that they want to be sure of their money. Some women report that when they say they are divorced (not widowed) they are turned down as tenants in such a way as to suggest that being divorced makes them unacceptable. Prejudice of this kind does persist in some quarters. One man, deserted by his wife and left with the children, reported that his landlord, when he got to know of the divorce, had asked him to quit. The father could have fought his eviction, but he did not know this at the time. Fortunately he had the means to pay a deposit on a new home, and did not have to move too far away. Leaving prejudice aside, there is the undeniable fact that where toddlers are learning to eat, to paint, to turn on taps in the bathroom and so on, the wear and tear on any property – especially furnished accommodation – may well be extensive. Some owners resolutely refuse to let flats or houses to tenants with young children, whether or not they are divorced.

If you are renting a home for the first time it will probably help to look at the various leaflets giving information about rents, tenants' rights, rates and so on, which are published from time to time by the Stationery Office and are obtainable from local Council Offices and from the Citizens' Advice Bureau. All areas have a Rent Officer whose job it is to deal with queries about privately rented accommodation. Tenancy agreements or leases are sometimes drawn up by solicitors, or by estate agents, and when this happens the landlord and the tenant each sign identical copies of the document; the tenant keeps the one signed by the landlord, and vice versa. It really is most important that you should fully understand what your tenancy agreement or lease says. Whatever happens, do not sign it without reading it, and if there is anything you do not understand, make sure you get professional advice about it. The liability for decoration and repairs, both internal and external, has to be carefully defined at the outset. There may be regulations about keeping pets, storing inflammable materials like paraffin, having window boxes, hanging out washing, that have to be noted. See that you know exactly what is involved before you sign the document, and have it vetted by a solicitor if you are in doubt. In cases where there is no formal lease or tenancy agreement the landlord is required by law to provide his tenants with a Rent Book in which payments of rent are recorded, and it is quite normal for a short form of tenancy agreement to be contained at the back of the book. This will state, among other things, whether or not the tenant may sub-let part or all of the accommodation. This is very important, for sub-letting is a possible source of extra income. If the agreement does not say that you may not sub-let, then you can do so.

Tenants of furnished accommodation have rather different rights from those of unfurnished properties. If an unfairly high rent is being charged, the local Rent Officer is the person to help. He can also deal with queries about your security as a tenant, and, as the law is frequently changed in its application to landlords and tenants, you should seek his advice if you are in doubt. It could be that yours is a case for the Rent Tribunal, which fixes rents and has the power to deal with some disputes between landlords and tenants.

The place to find details of houses and flats to let in your area is the local newspaper, or the estate agent's office, and there are sometimes shops that have advertisements in their windows giving details of available accommodation. Tradesmen can also sometimes help, knowing when a family is moving away. It can be worth your asking the milkman or grocer to keep a lookout and let you know of property that may be to let, or people who may be leaving. Some towns now have housing associations for unsupported mothers and their children; these associations generally own large houses which have been converted into flatlets, and include communal facilities for laundry and the like. Some of these schemes are privately run, others are organized by a charity and some come under the local Housing Authority. Council offices can supply details, and as schemes of this kind are increasing in number all the time it can be worth while asking if there are any operating in your area.

Quite a lot of people find that they can obtain a home by taking on a particular job. A telephonist told us that by signing on for night work she became eligible for the flat situated above a small telephone exchange where she worked. There are often caretakers' jobs available on the same terms, and when you cannot get help from the local Council or from agents in finding somewhere to live, a visit to the Labour Exchange may find you both a job and a home. Do not, however, take a job for which you are not trained, solely to get somewhere to live. This can lead to your being turned out fairly quickly, because this type of accommodation lasts only as long as the job does. One man who took a gardener's post in order to get a small cottage on an estate ended by losing both the job and the cottage when it turned out that he knew nothing about gardening.

We have already mentioned the local Council, and you will of course know that all Councils have accommodation that they let to people in their own areas. This is normally done on the basis of priorities, and there is usually some kind of 'points system', under which large families are more likely to receive accommodation than others. Names are usually put on a waiting list, and in many areas it may be years before your name comes to the top of the list. Some private tenants put their names on the list of the local Housing Authority, so as to stand a chance of getting Council accommodation one day.

Where a couple are living in a council house or flat and their marriage breaks up, the Housing Authority will often agree to transfer the tenancy from the name of the husband to that of the wife, if it is the husband who has left and she remains in occupation with the children. On the other hand, there have been cases in which local authorities have asked men to leave properties which they are occupying alone, having been left by their families. If a wife leaves a Council property there is little that the Council can then do to help her. Homeless people are legally the responsibility of the local authority in whose district they live and work, but the accommodation available for them is often as scarce as it is unpleasant. The authorities will usually do their best to find even temporary accommodation for homeless families, for if they do not do this the children may have to be taken into the care of the local authority, but the standards are often very low and no one wants to have to go into this type of accommodation if they can possibly avoid it.

Sometimes a husband or wife, left alone, or alone with the children, will go to friends or relatives who live in Council accommodation. This is allowed by Councils only as a temporary measure because they cannot allow their houses to become overcrowded, and their properties are not intended to be used as boarding houses. Failure of Council tenants to comply with regulations about overcrowding can lead to *both* families being given notice to quit. Some people trying to obtain Council accommodation, after seeing the local authority housing department without success, may try to speed things up by enlisting the support of a local councillor, their children's headmaster or perhaps their member of parliament. There is nothing to prevent you from doing this, but there is no point in expecting unfair preferential treatment. Nevertheless, the more people who know about your problem the better is your chance of finding somewhere to live, so it is well worth exploring every contact you have.

A few fortunate people are in a position to buy a house or flat of their own. This is usually easier for a man than a woman, because he will find it simpler to obtain a mortgage than she will. A wage-earning father is regarded by a Building Society –

or any mortgagee – as a better proposition than are the majority of wage-earning mothers. And at a time when mortgage money is scarce, lenders obviously tend to prefer borrowers who are most likely to be reliable. This means that a divorced woman – or any single woman – who wants to get a mortgage on a house must have a steady, salaried job, as a teacher or civil servant, for instance, or at least a reliable guarantor who will promise to make good her instalments if she fails to pay them, in order to satisfy a lender that she is a safe investment. Even to take on an existing mortgage from her husband can involve a divorced wife in a long, hard and losing battle. When their marriage broke up, Mr and Mrs M and their four children were living in a house which was privately mortgaged. In other words, the money had been loaned by an individual and not by a Building Society. Mr M wanted to sell the house, paying off the mortgage and dividing the remaining money between himself and his wife, which would leave each of them with about £1,000. Mr M could put his money immediately into another home, and indeed this was just what he planned to do, but she was in a different position. With four children and only maintenance payments on which to rely, she found that no Building Society would help her by taking over the loan. What would happen, they asked, if her husband died, lost his job or emigrated? How would she be able to ensure that the payments continued?

Mrs M was determined to keep her house somehow for the sake of her children who were all at school locally. She managed to borrow £1,000 and with this she bought her husband out, taking over the existing mortgage. The next part of her plan was to get the house to earn its keep by taking in paying guests, but this was not easy. Mr M had neglected the property; the roof leaked, repairs were desperately needed and there was scarcely room for extra people. Mrs M's bank agreed to make her a small loan, and with this she did the repairs and added an extra room. Then she let two rooms, got a part-time job, and just managed to keep up with her heavy financial commitments, which now included mortgage payments, bank interest and interest on the original £1,000 she had borrowed. Then the mortgagee died; the solicitors acting for his executors explained to Mrs M that, in order to pay death duties, they had to ask for repayment of the mortgage. No one could be found to supply another private mortgage, and so the house had to be sold after all. After a long struggle, Mrs M was finally without a home.

For most people who have become divorced or separated, finding a new home is one of their greatest problems. In the whole complicated business of families re-housing after divorce, two facts plainly emerge. For one, and often both partners, divorce brings a lower standard of living; and both of them may have to make several moves from one place to another before any settled and final home materializes.

Mrs N left her husband, taking with her their eight-year-old son. She first went to her parents, knowing that the arrangement could only be temporary as her parents were elderly and their house was too small for the whole family to share. After a few weeks, she took a job in another part of the country, and arranged for her son to go to a local school near where she worked. The plan sounded good, but it worked out badly; Mrs N was overworked and taken advantage of, and her health suffered. Desperate for any escape, she left and moved into rooms in the town, a sitting-room and bedroom for which she could only just afford to pay out of her small income, now much reduced because she had been able to find only a small part-time job. After a while the landlady said she could really only spare one room, and generally became awkward and disobliging. Mrs N's next move was to a small, partly furnished house, the best prospect so far. It belonged to an elderly woman who had gone to live with her son and daughter-in-law, and they acted for her in making the letting arrangements. In her enthusiasm, Mrs N spent what little money she had on improvements to the house, which had been empty for about six months, and did quite a lot of decorating. She had originally been granted a lease of a year, but had been told she would be able to renew the lease as the old lady was not likely to be able to go back there. But by the time the year was up, the old lady had gone into an old people's home, and her son was anxious to sell the house and have the capital. Mrs N could have taken the landlord to court, but she didn't. After her illness and all the worry about the divorce, she simply couldn't face it.

Mrs N then went to share a friend's flat, and had the added expense of storing her furniture. She did not want to part with it in case she later got the chance of renting somewhere unfurnished. The accommodation at the flat was good, but the arrangement included sharing a kitchen, and in time this became impossibly trying for them both. Finally, Mrs N found a flat of her own. Her son managed to get a place at a good local school, she found a job which she liked and where she was happy, and took her furniture out of store. But it had taken three years and six moves, as well as a vast amount of worry, trouble and expense to get there.

As we have mentioned, it is easier for a man to find accommodation than a woman. We talked to six men about the way in which they coped after their marriages had broken up:

Mr O left his wife and moved into a bed-sitting room in the town where he worked. The place was rather depressing and pokey, but it was the best he could afford after paying maintenance to his wife.

Mr P, deserted by his wife, gave up his council house, took his children and went home to his widowed mother, who took them all in and looked after them. He pronounced himself 'better looked after than I ever was by my wife' and, although the house was on the small side, the arrangement had many advantages over any other he could have made.

Mr Q left his wife and moved into a house rented by a woman. Later on, he married her.

Mr R took a bachelor flat where he lived and looked after himself until he remarried and his new wife moved in with him.

Mr S worked in a hospital and, having left his wife, went to live on the job.

Mr T arranged for the matrimonial home to be sold after his wife and children left him, and emigrated. The proceeds of the sale were divided between himself and his wife, and he started a new life on the other side of the world.

A bed-sitter, a lonely flat, a sleeping bag on the office floor, or a big empty house may not be ideal, but the fact is that some form of accommodation can always be found by a single man who has a job. By the same token, if he decides or is forced to make a change, he will have less difficulty in finding somewhere else to go than will a woman with children. The divorced man with children is rarely homeless, for he is not given care of the children by the court unless he has already shown that suitable accommodation and adequate help are available. Also, the figure of the deserted male left to look after the children is one that attracts sympathetic assistance from every quarter. Why is it that the deserted woman in exactly the same predicament is less appealing to our society? Is it that we expect the mother to look after her children, come what may? Do we say to ourselves, 'Well, he may have left, but he is still liable to support her, so what is she worrying about?' This assumption could not be more wrong, in the great majority of cases.

While society sees what has happened to a couple, it knows nothing of their feelings. And yet, even when the practical adjustments of one's living – or housing – standards have been made, for better or worse, there are still the feelings of people to be considered. Anxious mothers, for instance, wonder how the children will feel about moving with them to a small flat after living in a moderately large house with a pleasant garden. And one hears of fathers who take their children out on access days, but are careful not to let them see the small bed-sitter that they now have to occupy. Then there is the effect on morale of a lowered standard of living. How can a woman be proud of a damp, dark basement if she has been used to a light, airy house? And is it worth decorating rooms when the future is so uncertain that you may have to move out in six months, or even three?

Thousands of people have nowhere to live at all. If you have somewhere, count yourself lucky and concentrate on what is positive and good about it. Does it suit your circumstances? Can you afford it, bearing in mind the heating and running costs? Can you improve it – either by hard work or by thinking out ways round the snags and discomforts? Or do you feel you could do better somewhere else? We say more about the pros and cons of moving house in Chapter 7, but here we would suggest that for your own sake you try not to let moving become a habit. Move only if you have to, or if you are sure that it is a move for the better.

CHAPTER 5

Getting Help

How to get help? What kind of help? Ours is a strange island; one can sometimes think that there are more people trying to give help than those needing it. And yet there are large gaps between the demand and the services available. Although we have a Welfare Society, with many statutory social services available to help families, it can happen that three or four of these services are supporting the same family, each ignorant of the work of the others. It was realized some time ago that this did not make sense, and the Government decided to set up local Departments of Social Service so that one Family Service could be established. These are steadily being developed, but in the meantime you have to know what different services there are, what they can and cannot do and where they are to be found.

It was thought by some people, when the Welfare State became a reality, that there would be little if any future need for voluntary organizations offering personal help, counsel and advice, but this was not what happened. Today there are still any number of voluntary agencies helping people with marriage problems, with suicidal feelings, with alcoholism, housing, unwanted pregnancies and so on. It has always been the voluntary agencies which have tried to fill the gaps left in the social welfare system. Some fade away after a time, their purpose fulfilled; others become so vital that they are taken over, financed and staffed by the State.

Then there are the professionals, individuals who have had many years of training and experience before gaining their qualifications. They do not usually operate as large organizations, but tend to work in small groups, in partnership, or individually. Such is the status of the professions that many people like to adopt the title 'professional' to describe themselves, their work and their attitude to it. What is important, of course, is the quality of the work they do, and the degree of skill and understanding they bring to it. On the whole, one can reckon that the fewer the claims made by members of the professions the more competent they really are.

Your first problem, having selected the service or the person whose help you think you need, is to get in touch with them. For the self-confident, this is a fairly simple task – they simply write or telephone for an appointment, or just turn up and ask for what they want. But for many more, it is not so easy. You may lack the words to say what help you think you want, or may be ashamed of having to ask at all. You may be frightened that, if you cannot express yourself clearly and say exactly what you need, you may be dismissed as a fool. Yet it is our experience that the really competent social workers and professionals understand these fears very well, and realize it to be part of their job to help people to say what they mean or what they want, using their own words. To be prompted with the right question at the right moment makes you feel both understood and reassured.

Of course, some social workers and professionals are better than others. Some are only partly trained, and others still inexperienced. Others have personal problems of their own that come between them and the service they are trying to give. Mrs V, separated for three years from her husband, became pregnant. She did not want to marry the father of the child, and was in two minds about adoption. This was her first pregnancy, and after some half-hearted attempts at an abortion, she decided to have the baby. Half the time she felt that she ought to keep the baby when it came; but sometimes she was overcome by guilt and a feeling that she could never look after it properly. She went to a voluntary organization that had homes in different parts of the country and, after meeting a sympathetic social worker employed by them, arranged to go to a home some weeks before the baby was due. When she eventually got there, fearful of what would happen, she was met by the matron, who explained the rules. Mrs V was told she would nurse the baby for several weeks after the birth, and when she said that this worried her because she would get fond of the child, the matron replied, 'Well, you got yourself into this, didn't you?'

The matron had never married, and in a way she was punishing girls for having had the sex she had never enjoyed, and so obviously flaunting it by becoming pregnant. This story is true; but however much we say that a woman of that kind should not have been allowed anywhere near the home, we cannot alter the fact that she was there, nor that many others are like her. Just as there are many like the social worker who first saw and helped Mrs V, so there are a few like the matron. What can you do about it? In the first place, try not to be too surprised at the reactions of other people. We are not trying to tell you that they will all react unpleasantly; they will not. But just as you bring your feelings and attitudes to the interview, so they bring theirs. They are men and women like yourself, endowed possibly with more skill and knowledge, but not essentially better or worse than you are. If some – a minority – of them behave in a way that you find worrying or distressing, see them as people with their own difficulties rather than as fiendish adversaries out to thwart you.

We will start by describing the work of the professions and of related occupations, and medicine is the obvious place to start. Almost everyone has at some time a need to consult his doctor. You will probably have done so yourself on more than one occasion, and many people in the throes of a separation or a divorce find that they need some kind of medical help during the times when they are most distressed. It is surprising how often people say, 'I couldn't ask my doctor – he has known me ever since I was a child, and I simply couldn't tell him about this.' Although understandable, this attitude is completely mistaken. Firstly, he has almost certainly come across your problem many times before, and is not at all shocked by learning the disclosures that for you are entirely personal and private. Secondly, you need his help, you are entitled to it, and you should take advantage of it. With all its inadequacies, we are blessed with a National Health Service that costs you very little, or nothing at all if you have a low income.

It is most important to treat the doctor in a reasonable way, to arrive at his surgery in good time, and to explain your difficulty as briefly as possible. Treat him as a person whose time is valuable, but who has both the skill and the patience to support you if you first explain your problem and then follow his advice. If he says you are to take some tablets regularly for three weeks, then do not give up after ten days when you begin to feel better. Get his help when you first feel ill rather than calling him at a weekend or in the night. Once he knows you are the kind of patient who will ask for help only when you need it, he will be glad to see you.

Others can help with physical problems of a different nature. The oculist will be consulted over any difficulty about your eyesight, and the dentist regarding your mouth and teeth. With both these people, and indeed with any professional person, be sure that you go for help when the problem first starts to worry you, and not at the last moment. By leaving your teeth until they need to be taken out, or by straining your eyes unnecessarily, you make extra work for the dentist and the oculist, give yourself discomfort, and probably affect your appearance too.

The most valuable thing the professional has to offer is his time. This applies also to lawyers, and to the clergy. We discussed the role of the lawyer at some length in Chapter 2, but what of the clergy? The position of a priest or minister is today very different from what it was fifty or even twenty years ago, when churches were attended by more people more regularly than they are today. Many clergy complain, and with good reason, that the only use some people want to make of them is to officiate at weddings, funerals and christenings. We do not suggest that there are no individual churchgoers today, nor that all parsons are out of touch with the people – church or non-church – who live in their parishes. Nevertheless it must be recognized that our society as a whole has emphatically rejected, for good or ill, the paternal authority of the church, and in doing so it has tended to reject the parson too, with all he has to offer.

Well, what has he to offer you? Clergymen know what it is to have problems in human relationships, management and, most of all, money, for they are paid notoriously low salaries, and both they and their wives understand very well the practical difficulties of making ends meet. Most men who go into the church do so because they want to offer some kind of help and support to other people. By caring what happens to you and being prepared to listen, a clergyman has something really valuable to offer even if you neither share nor want to share his particular religious faith.

It can be the same with members of his congregation. We know, of course, that some of them will not feel this way. There are a few church organizations even now whose rules forbid membership to divorced people. In rural areas especially, where church and village are still closely bound together socially, the application of such a rule can prove extremely wounding to the person concerned. But it is a rule and that is that. The unfortunate thing, as we have said elsewhere in this book, is that people who feel rejected by their marriage partner tend to feel rejected by everyone else. Rejection by a church organization which has to abide by its rules is more than anything else a technical matter – the policy of the organization. It does not mean rejection on a personal level by all its members, the entire Christian Church, or God himself. Nevertheless, to some people that is how it feels. And it takes a degree of toughness not found in the emotionally wounded to overlook rejection in one place and seek acceptance in another. The chances are that they will take no more risks, but turn instead somewhat savagely on whoever or whatever it was that set their wounds smarting again. It is a pity. There are as many fantastic images of divorced men and women as there are of parsons and churchgoers. Either group presents a challenge to the other, and intercommunication between them, when it happens, is a triumph for both sides.

There could be all sorts of reasons why you might feel reluctant about seeking a minister's help. For one thing, there is a strong possibility that he will talk about God, and many people who have no other conversational taboos dislike this or find it embarrassing and inappropriate. Then it may be that you have not worked out the morality of what you are doing, are not sure about it and do not want to be asked disturbing questions that make it all seem more painful than it does already. But the clergyman, counsellor, lawyer or friend who helps you to face your feelings really is doing you a service, provided he does not take up a moral stance of his own by telling you how to behave. Perhaps you hesitate to approach a priest because you had a strong religious upbringing, have since altered your views, and do not now want to be reminded of past conflicts and uncertainties. Or perhaps you had an anti-religious upbringing and it does not occur to you that the parish priest may be a useful person; perhaps you do know him, or he has not been useful in the past.

A clergyman, too, may be in a difficult position because his church is deeply divided in its attitude to divorce, and if you are going to discuss this with him, it might be as well to start by finding out whether he takes a stand on the issue. Some Church of England clergy have a most sympathetic and imaginative attitude towards divorced people who ask their help; some even think that a form of remarriage in church should be available in certain cases, whereas others have come out fiercely and volubly against such a suggestion. Two-thirds of all first marriages still take place in church though far less than this proportion of the population go there regularly. One reason for having reservations about seeing a clergyman regarding a marriage problem s that you may have promised in the marriage service to take your partner 'for better for worse', and he may tell you that this means what it says. Certainly there is no denying the fact that the clergyman, unlike the doctor or the solicitor from whom you also take advice, does represent a doctrine, and his views and actions are bound in some ways to reflect it. Either because of it – or you may think in spite of it – he may be able to help you, so count him among your possible sources of help.

A point worth remembering is that the vicar usually knows about clubs and organizations which exist in his parish, as well as knowing the people involved with them. If you have moved recently or want to be put in touch with local activities, he may be a useful contact. Even if you have lived in the same area for some time, it is likely that the vicar will know a great many more local people than you do, and could well be the person best able to find you an answer to questions like 'Do you know anyone who . . .

could babysit for me?

wants a bed-sitting room in my flat?
has a couple of rooms to let?
needs some part-time secretarial work done?
would like help with nursing a relative?
will darn my socks?'

You might try to forget about his dog-collar and see whether he can in fact help. He might put you in touch with the Company of Compassion, which is linked with the Mothers' Union and can sometimes offer holidays for tired mothers in need of a rest, or arrange for you to have a home with someone else.

In Victorian times 'the Professions' were the Law, Medicine and the Church, but today we look for skilled help of a similar standard from many others. Accountants, teachers, stockbrokers, bankers, insurance brokers, estate agents and others have expertise which we need and can use. In Chapter 3 we discussed the help a banker can give and explained how your accountant can sort out your income-tax affairs to your best advantage. Accountants do many other types of work, such as handling the accounts of large and small businesses, advising on the best ways of raising loans, and so on. You may be unlikely to come across a stockbroker, for not many people who become divorced or separated have much money to put aside for investment, but if you were to come into a legacy or sell a house, having several thousand pounds in the bank as a result, you should certainly consider the best way to invest this, and here a stockbroker will be able to help you. Different people have different needs. A woman with three children to bring up needs the highest possible income from any money she has, provided the investment is safe. A man with a reasonable income, due to retire in ten years or so, is looking for an investment that will grow in value during that time, and is not much worried about the income meanwhile; but when his retirement comes he will expect his stockbroker to give him new advice about his investments. An accountant charges a fee on the basis of the amount of work he does, while a stockbroker gets a scale commission on every transaction he makes, sale or purchase.

The role of your child's teacher will be considered in Chapter 8, but something needs to be said concerning insurance brokers and estate agents. If you own a car or a house, if you need to protect your family against the risk of your premature death, if you have valuable jewellery or a small business, then you need insurance. An insurance broker is there to offer help. He finds out what you need, then gets the best bargain he can by looking at the 'rates' offered by the various insurance companies. Make sure, though, that you are recommended to an insurance broker by someone you trust, such as your bank manager or solicitor. This also applies in the case of estate agents. There are some highly reputable estate agents whose firms have operated in their areas for a century or more, but there are others who have no qualifications and are interested only in the commission they can get on a sale, irrespective of the adequacy of the price or the suitability of the house to the buyer. Fortunately, they are in a small minority, but obviously one should steer clear of them, and again it is best to get the help of an estate agent through responsible recommendation. He will sell your house, or help you to buy one. When selling, there is no reason why you should not ask the opinion of more than one agent, but you should also get some idea of the value of the house yourself, by studying the advertisements in the local press. When buying, you really have to look after yourself, because the agent is acting for the seller, and not for you. He will charge his commission to the seller, and his job is to get the best price he can. He need not tell you of any defects, such as dry rot or a faulty electrical system, although he cannot deliberately mislead you. Agents will also let properties; some firms specialize in this sort of work more than others, so again it is best to act on recommendation, or at least by reference to the local press.

We have already mentioned doctors, but there are a host of other workers in the general medical field who may be able to help you from time to time. Some of them have specific medical training, others have not, but you need to know what they do and how they can help you. We will consider the functions of the Health Visitor, the Medical Social Worker, the Psychiatric Social Worker, the Mental Welfare Officer, the Hospitals, and also of Home Helps.

First the Health Visitor. She visits every home where there is a new baby, and she is the key worker to give help to parents with children under the age of five. A Health Visitor has had the basic training of a nurse, and also has qualifications in midwifery. She knows what other social services are available in your area, and can put you in touch with the people concerned, having met or spoken with them fairly frequently. A Health Visitor is employed by the County or the County Borough Council, and may be attached to a group of local doctors. You can get her address from your doctor's surgery, the local Council or a Health Clinic; and the sort of situation in which you will ask for her help is when you are worried about the health of one of your children.

Mrs W had two small sons. One was plump and healthy and seemed more or less unconcerned about Daddy's absence, making good relationships with many people and getting a lot of friendly attention. The other boy, though older, was developing much more slowly. He had spoken very little by the age of three-and-a-half, and his few words were difficult to understand. He would not talk to strangers, and was subject to violent fits of temper. Mrs W mentioned this to her doctor, who asked the Health Visitor to call. This she did, and realized that there was nothing seriously wrong with the boy. It occurred to her that he really needed the company of other children, with less competition from his obviously popular small brother. She felt that his disturbance was at least partly due to Mrs W's own anxiety, and spoke to the woman in charge of a local nursery school. He was found a place there, at first only in the mornings and later for the afternoons as well, and he improved very quickly. Mrs W had expected tantrums, but after only two days he settled down and was soon speaking much better. The Health Visitor, by knowing what local facilities were available, had given her exactly the help she needed.

Medical Social Workers were once referred to as Almoners. They are attached to hospitals and have many responsibilities there for seeing to the personal rather than the medical needs of patients. Like the Health Visitor, the Medical Social Worker can mobilize the other community resources to help you. She will have had social work training. If you have been in hospital, are there now, or expect to go there soon for treatment, she is the person to see about any kind of practical help you need, e.g. looking after the children, or getting help around the house.

Hospitals are places that most of us know little about. Even the patient only sees a small part of the activity that keeps these enormous establishments running. Quite apart from medical services, there are staff to be housed, people to be fed, records to be made and filed, buildings to be heated and roads, corridors, wards and rooms to be cleaned. Hospital administration has now become something of a profession on its own account so complex is the total task. Why are we telling you this? Because if you or your children have to go into hospital for some reason you will inevitably find the set-up puzzling. Rules are made which you find hard to understand and harder to like. Usually they are reasonable in all the circumstances, but if you really have got a serious complaint then you can always make contact with the local Hospital Management Committee. Incidentally, if you have to visit hospital regularly from time to time and cannot afford the fare, the Department of Health and Social Security will help.

People who have mental illness, a common though often temporary condition, have many sources of help available as well as those provided by their own doctor. There are Mental Welfare Officers, working for the Health Department of the local Council. The Mental Welfare Officer is the person to call if you cannot get your doctor's help and if someone is behaving in a very strange way and may need to be admitted to hospital. Also, and doing rather similar work in some respects, there are Psychiatric Social Workers who have had a training of some length and are usually attached to hospitals. They are not only there to help the mentally disturbed before and after they have been in hospital, but also to give support to the family of the patient. This is a most important function, as the odd behaviour of people with a mental illness can be both distressing and frightening to their families. These workers help to allay such feelings by explaining what is happening and how they can help.

There are a host of other ancillary medical services. Local

Councils employ nurses who can work full-time in the home. They can also supply you with a Home Help, though these are in very short supply and are usually kept to help old people or those who are ill or who have just had a baby. Councils also employ midwives, and operate health centres where you can get cheap (or sometimes free) foods for children. There are also ante-natal clinics and specialist clinics, e.g. for mental illness, tuberculosis and so on. Now and again there may be in your area a radiography unit which will check your health by taking X-rays, or an immunization unit, especially when an epidemic has arrived or is expected. Your own doctor, or the local Council Health Department, will let you know what is available and where. Even if you make contact with the wrong Council department at first this does not matter very much, though of course it is easier if you start in the right place. If you meet a surly or overtired official, you are more likely to get the answer you want if you remain polite, and behave as if the other person had not been rude or offensive.

Next, you need to know what Statutory Services can do for you. These are the services which the Government and local Councils are legally obliged to provide. They are staffed in the main by social workers, a fairly new group of people who have a form of training that not only equips them to give advice and practical help, but also to offer understanding and a kind of personal support that is more human than official. Some of them, of course, are better than others at this work, but most have had intensive training for their job. Others, mostly in the older age group, may have had less training but are more experienced. The title 'social worker' covers a multitude of occupations and interests, and is not in itself a qualification.

We have already described the functions of the Department of Health and Social Security in our chapter on Money, Chapter 3. One of its main functions is to deal with claims for supplementary benefits, that is, for cash payments to those who are in severe financial need. They also give information and advice about pension entitlements, sickness benefit, maternity and death payments and so on. The Department's office is fairly easy to find, and when you go in you will see someone sitting behind an inquiry desk. Normally this official will not be able to give you detailed help with your problem, so you should explain what you want quite simply. If this is your first visit you will then probably have a private interview with another official in a small room nearby, not in the main waiting room. The official is there to explain your legal position so far as benefits and entitlement are concerned, and will probably offer you leaflets that explain your rights in more detail. He may help you fill in an application form. He or she is empowered to offer emergency help if this is what you need, but if the problem facing you is not urgent it will probably be wise to consider your position carefully for a few days before deciding what to do. If you do not quite understand the alternatives open to you, don't hesitate to go back for a further explanation, or pay a visit to the Citizens' Advice Bureau and ask someone there to explain your position to you.

Most towns also have a Labour Exchange, and if you have not found the job you are looking for in the columns of the local press, or if you first want advice on what types of work will best suit you and are available locally, you should visit the Exchange. Its rather strange name in fact implies that both employers and potential employees can 'register' there and be put in touch with one another. Nobody can force you to take any job you do not want, and a visit to the Labour Exchange does not oblige you to start on any particular date or in any particular place. The Exchange merely provides a useful service that some time you may need.

You may well think of the Probation Service as concerned exclusively with criminal matters, and indeed a lot of their work is now with discharged prisoners and people who have been put 'on probation' by the Courts. This is not the only work they do. If a parent, for instance, considers that his child is getting out of hand and may be involved in some criminal activity, it is quite all right to get in touch with the Probation Officer. An alternative which many people prefer, though, is to see a Child Care Officer, and the Child Care Service is now doing much of the work that Probation Officers used to do. In many areas, Probation Officers are well known for their capacity to help with marriage difficulties, and people who have met them or heard of their work may turn to them rather than to the Marriage Guidance Council. Divorce Court Welfare Officers, whose work we mention in Chapter 8 on Children, are recruited from the Probation Service.

For families who have ceased to be able to cope with home life, with the ordinary work of cooking, housekeeping and so on, there are in many of the larger towns Family Service Units. The workers attached to these units are trained not only for general social work but also for tough manual work of the most practical kind. They often show mothers how to cook, how to cope with management of the house and of children, and work out a weekly budget. Their service is not really for people who can solve their problems in a normal way, and they should only be asked for help when things are very much out of control.

The Statutory Services do not give answers to all your practical problems. They will help in the ways we have described, but you will find from time to time that they either cannot or will not help with some difficulty that is outside their legal responsibility. Often this is a matter of approach; when Mr X went for an interview at the Department of Health and Social Security about the stamp he should put on his Insurance Card while he was self-employed, he first complained loudly because he had been kept waiting. He then objected to having to explain his story to a woman, saying he would prefer to discuss matters with a man. As it happened, he had recently left his job because of a row with the manager of the firm, and he was doing casual work for the time being. This entitled him to apply to the Magistrates' Court for an alteration in the amount of his maintenance payment to his wife. By the time he had gracelessly accepted the interview with a woman who told him his responsibilities regarding National Insurance he was in a worse temper. She was in no mood to offer him any help beyond that which she had to give as part of her job. Mr X asked how he could apply to the Magistrates. Although she knew very well how this could be done, she merely said she could not help, with an icy apology. He went away and did nothing about it until he got into real trouble with the maintenance payments. Had he known, he could easily have gone direct to the Magistrates' Clerk for help.

Even the most helpful social worker cannot provide the answers to some problems, and may recommend people to visit a voluntary organization which gives a non-statutory service, such as the Marriage Guidance Council, the Samaritans, the Salvation Army and others. We have several times mentioned the work of the Citizens' Advice Bureaux, of which there are over four hundred in this country. You can find their addresses in the telephone book, from the Post Office, the local Council offices or the Police. The Bureaux are staffed partly by volunteers and partly by paid staff, and they can give you help with many practical problems. They specialize in rental problems, also hire purchase difficulties and disputes with shops about goods that have been bought. If you think your rent is too high, or the landlord is expecting you to do something that you believe is not covered in the lease, the Citizens' Advice Bureau is the right place to go. The Bureaux often have lawyers available to give free advice, and their workers have useful handbooks to guide them through the maze of laws that relate to rented accommodation, hire purchase and the sale of goods. So it is worth seeing them if you have a problem over the payments you owe on H.P. for furniture, a car or anything else. If you want to stop the payments and give the goods back, this may be possible, and the Citizens' Advice Bureaux can advise you.

Other problems they cover are matrimonial difficulties, especially financial disputes and arguments over property, though if these are complex you will naturally need the help of a lawyer. They can give advice about other financial matters, and one of their most useful functions is not only to offer direct help and advice, but to see that you are referred to the right service specializing in your kind of problem. So they may suggest that a client sees a marriage counsellor, visits the Family Planning Association, the Department of Health and Social Security and so on. If you are in doubt about which service, statutory, voluntary or professional you should consult, see the Citizens' Advice Bureau, who will make no charge for their advice. These Bureaux were first set up during the 1939–1945 war, to aid citizens with the many problems created by wartime legislation, and were found to be so valuable that they have kept going ever since. They are voluntarily run, but do receive local authority money.

Remember that the voluntary organizations are not obliged to set up in any area, and this may mean that you have to go some way for the help you need. Not only this, but there is inevitably some variation in the quality of the service offered. Naturally there are social workers of differing skills and experience, but they all have the training and qualifications for the paid work they do. The calibre of the men and women in the voluntary organizations tends to vary more widely. Although there are some first-class people offering support of the highest standard, there are others who are not doing at all a good job, but who happen to be the only people available. A word or two with someone who knows the neighbourhood can often sort out the sheep from the goats for you. If a service is not available nearby, or if the particular sheep you see is no help to you, don't give up altogether. Nearly always there is some person or agency able to cope with your problem, and painstaking inquiry of the local police, probation officers, shopkeepers or clergy will often turn up your answer. If there happens to be a Council of Social Service in your area, they may be able to help. If the service you need is too far away, suggest to that Council that something should be done about it, for one of their jobs is to find out what is missing locally and to try to fill the gap. Now and again the Council of Social Service can put you in touch with a club or other group or society who can help you.

Some people think that Marriage Guidance Councils are just not interested in helping people who have been divorced or separated. Mrs Y had been told that marriage counsellors couldn't help unless husband and wife came along together, and that because she was divorced they would refuse to see her about a difficulty she had in her relationship with a man she had been living with and who wanted to marry her. She was quite unable to decide whether she wanted to marry him or not. She had been badly hurt once, and was scared of another disaster, but at the same time she thought this might be her only chance of security. While she was wondering about this she saw an article in the local paper explaining that marriage counsellors often saw single people, and did not insist on a visit from both husband and wife. She had to wait quite a long time for an appointment and was distressed and irritated by this, not realizing that marriage counsellors work part-time and are not paid; this is why it sometimes takes a few weeks to get an appointment.

At last she found herself in the Marriage Guidance Council waiting room, expecting to see some worthy lady ready to dispense words of good advice. She was surprised to find a youngish woman her own age, and in many ways rather like her. She returned for several interviews. Although the counsellor did not tell her whether or not she should marry the man she was living with, she ultimately made up her mind that she would. Her worries, she decided, were based not so much on his character as on her former husband's. It was so refreshing to talk all this over with someone who was prepared to listen for an hour at a time, who did not disapprove of what she was doing, but who in fact became quite a friend. It was a friendship that existed only in the counselling rooms, however, and in fact Mrs Y never found out where the counsellor lived, or what her home background was like. In fact, the counsellor's husband was an engineer, she had two children at school, and was able to give some time to this counselling work. She had been one of three people selected as councillors out of ten who had applied locally to help the Marriage Guidance Council. After a two-year period of training, all taken in her spare time, she was now seeing several people a week, and receiving professional supervision and guidance herself. There are men counsellors too, and you can ask to see either a man or a woman. An appointment can be made by telephoning the Appointments Secretary of the Marriage Guidance Council, whose number will be in the telephone book. There are about one hundred and twenty such Councils throughout the country, and they get their financial support from private donations, from local Councils and from a government grant. Clients are not asked to pay anything but a small registration fee, and all interviews are completely confidential.

This issue of confidentiality is most important, not only to Marriage Guidance Councils but also to all professional people and social workers. It would be quite impossible to expect people to seek help with intimate personal problems if they could not rely on the discretion of the person they were seeing, and it is therefore very much part of the training and the attitude of all who give this kind of help to keep the confidences of their clients.

Another very large national voluntary organization is the Family Planning Association. Under the terms of recent legislation, local Councils have the power to provide family planning facilities. Many are now doing this, and frequently making use of the existing services already being provided by the Family Planning Association, taking them over or paying the local Association for the service they give. The family planning clinics give contraceptive advice, and this is not now restricted to those who are married. The contraceptive pill is now the most popular method used, but other techniques are also advised to suit the individuals concerned. A small fee has normally to be paid, but this can be waived in the case of financial hardship. All the contraceptive advice is given by doctors or nurses but other jobs, such as making appointments, are done by volunteers or by staff who have no specific medical qualification. Details of booklets giving information about contraception are given on p. 195.

Some divorced and separated people have considerable problems with their parents. It can easily happen that an older man or woman is left alone, partially incapacitated in one way or another, and the only available help is from a son or daughter who already has more than enough of his or her own problems, following a marriage breakdown. In every district there is an Old People's Welfare organization and you can find their address from the local Council offices, the Citizens' Advice Bureau, a Health Centre or some other source.

Mrs Z was at her wit's end with an old aunt who had a little income but who seemed quite unable to cope with life. Periodically she had fits of forgetfulness, getting lost on the way home from shopping, or leaving her bag with all her money and food in a bus or on the counter of a shop. The old lady, before moving near her niece, had been closely connected with a church, and in the end it was found possible for the local church of the same denomination to find her a place to live. Her niece was able to inspect it first, and the old lady was perfectly happy there. Mrs Z had made contact with the church through the local Old People's Welfare Committee.

If you have only met members of the Salvation Army playing trumpets on street corners you may not be aware of all the other things they do. They have a remarkably effective service, known as the Missing Persons Bureau, which enables one spouse to trace another who has left home. In addition, they are willing to turn their hands to any number of difficult and often unpleasant jobs, expecting no reward.

You have also probably heard of the Samaritans, who were set up to help people in despair, especially those tempted to suicide. There are several branches of this organization, which has fairly close connections with the churches, and their general rule is to see that a telephone is available and manned twenty-four hours a day. They charge no fee, and will not preach at you.

For those plagued with the problem of drink, particularly if this is serious, there are many branches of the excellent organization, Alcoholics Anonymous, whose members help one another in a very practical and down-to-earth way. Also there are organizations offering help with drug addiction.

If you are unable to find the addresses of the many, many large and small organizations to help you with your problem, try writing to the readers' service of one of the big newspapers. The *Daily Mirror* and the *News of the World* offer what are probably the best services of this kind, but women's magazines also employ large staffs just to answer readers' questions and put them in touch with the right kind of help. You can write to your MP too, or go to see him if he is one of those who regularly sets aside time to help his constituents in this way. He can sometimes assist if you have come up against some problem with a large organization or service.

If you do not find the help you want in this chapter, then look through the reading list at the end of the book, or visit the local library for information about your own area. Ask people for help, and if you do not get it from the first person you approach, try not to be put off. Somewhere there is the person or the service that you need. If you succeed in finding them you may later be able to direct others to the same source.

CHAPTER 6

Managing

One major problem will be the management of the practical aspects of ordinary life that you may have left to your partner in the past. A man may have no experience of cooking his own meals, washing his clothes, or of buying the things he needs. A woman may have no idea what sort of bills to expect, how to make sure she has enough money to pay for them, how to deal with things that go wrong in the house, or how to cope with aggressive salesmen.

These problems are real, and they are worrying. You may take some time to get used to them, to find a way of coping; but be reassured, for most people who have to cope with these problems find that, in the end, they manage somehow. It is the first months that are so hard, when you already may be feeling desperately lonely and unable to meet and talk to people, or to ask their help. You are in a state of shock, so you keep forgetting where you have put things. You may go out to shop but be unable to remember what you wanted to buy; if you are not careful you can come home with all the wrong things and leave your change on the counter.

Let us start with the two most important ways of solving your practical problems: sorting out your priorities, and making a plan to deal with them. If there is simply not enough money to buy everything you need, or not enough time to deal with everything that needs doing, then this is a fact of life that cannot be changed. It must be faced, and part of facing it is making the decisions about what matters most. It can help to start with a blank sheet of paper. Write down the things you need, the jobs that ought to be done. Then put them down in order of importance. This can work out something like this:

Mrs A lives in a small flat with her two children, both of whom are at school. She receives a small amount of maintenance, but she needs new clothes and the children must have winter coats. Then there is the rent she must go on paying to the Council, and bills are starting to come in for gas and electricity. Her daughter has a birthday coming up, and there are the regular payments on the furniture in the living-room. There are other bills, too, for the newspaper, for the hire of TV and radio. And the children expect the same pocket money that they were getting before Mrs A and her husband separated. She knows that the telephone bill will come soon, and there are school meals to pay for every week. What savings she has in the Post Office, and there is very little left, will last only another two or three weeks at the most. Her father has offered to help if he can. This is the way that Mrs A's list – or budget – might look:

Out		*In*	
Food	£... per week	Maintenance	
Clothes for children	About £...	payments	£...
Clothes for me	About £...	Salary	£...
Chemist	£... per week	Family	
Rent	£... per week	allowance	£...
Gas bill	£...	Post Office	£...
Electricity bill	£...	Help from Father?	
Daughters' birthday present	£...		
HP on furniture	£... a month		
Hire of TV	£... a month		
Newspapers	... per week		
Pocket money for children	... per week		
School meals	... per week		

What are Mrs A's priorities? The rent must be paid, the children must be fed and clothed, she must eat too, and there must be some warmth in the house. These are the real priorities, and if the money coming in, which fortunately includes Mrs A's rather small wage for part-time work, is not enough to cope with them, she will probably need help from the Department of Health and Social Security (see Chapter 5). With luck, her income will cover more than these basic things; there may be enough to keep up the payments on the furniture, or on the TV. Probably, though, the telephone will have to be taken away, the children may have to do without pocket money and even without some presents. Mrs A may have to cancel the newspaper and give up her hopes of a new suit for herself. Possibly she will ask her father for some help, if not for herself at least for the children. If there is no alternative she may have to let some of the furniture be taken away, and to buy a small but safe paraffin heater to do the work of the much more expensive electric fires.

All these difficult and unpleasant decisions will have to be taken one way or another. If they are not planned on the basis of a list of priorities then the wrong things may go first. Mrs A will worry more if she finds that there is not enough money left to feed the children than if they have to do without the telephone; but if she has used her last few pounds on keeping the telephone connected, this may prevent her from getting the new coats that the children simply must have.

Here she may be able to cut down on cost by buying from a children's 'budget' or second-hand shop or maybe visiting a good jumble sale. Most large towns now have shops where outgrown clothes in good condition can be sold and bought. Schools often have schemes whereby uniforms can be obtained second-hand at much reduced cost. Nearly new clothes that originally cost rather a lot are sometimes advertised in local papers or on newsagents' windows. It is worth while watching for these advertisements and following them up if they sound promising. Someone with whom you can trade children's clothes regularly can be very useful. Be rather cautious about dealing with mail order firms, for it is easy to order from these more goods than you can really afford.

Now let us suppose that Mr A is living on his own. He has to pay her more maintenance than he feels he can afford, he tends to run out of money before the week is over. This means that he has started to borrow from friends, and they are getting less and less keen to lend to him. He feels that he wants to enjoy life at least some of the time, and of course this means he has to spend money. He eats tinned or frozen food most of the time, and has not really cooked himself a full meal since they separated.

Mr A has just as great a need to settle his priorities. He has to make the regular maintenance payments to Mrs A, and he must pay his own rent. He needs to eat and to travel to and from work, to have his shoes repaired, and to replace outworn clothes. These are the real priorities, and if he makes a list of them, among others, he will soon find out what he can manage to buy over and above the basic essentials. Maybe there will be enough left over for some extras, but not for all. Let us look at Mr A's list:

Out		*In*
Maintenance	£... a week	Salary £... a week
Rent	£... a week	
Fares	£... a week	
Food	£... a week	
Shoe repairs	£...	
New suit	£...	
Loans to pay back	£...	
Electricity meter	£... a week	
Cigarettes and drink	£...	

This is where planning comes in. If Mr A can manage to put aside a small sum of money each week he may soon have enough to pay for the new suit, or for the expense involved in taking out a woman he met recently and whom he likes. If he is willing to spend some part of the weekend looking round the shops instead of buying the tinned foods or frozen vegetables he can cook easily, he may be able to save quite a lot each week. If he buys drip-dry clothes when he needs them instead of clothes that take a lot of ironing, if he stays away from the social session that he knows will involve him in spending more than he can afford, then he should be able to get at least some of the things he wants. If he is prepared to try to cook for himself then again he will discover that it is cheaper this way, and after he has got over the worry about what his friends would think he may even be rather proud of this new skill. This will need careful thought, it may involve asking other people for their advice, and there will certainly be moments of embarrassment and of wondering whether it is all worth while. But it is possible to manage, as many men have proved.

Mrs A needs to plan as well. She may find that if she keeps the money in different boxes each week she will be able to allot the right amount of cash to food, clothes, rent and so on, and plan for paraffin and other things she needs. If the gas bill comes in once a quarter, then her best plan will be to divide the likely amount of the bill by thirteen, and put that amount aside each week until it comes in, by which time she will have enough to pay for it. She may need to save to buy clothes, as well. Or if she used to know how to use a sewing machine, then she might take advantage of her father's offer to help and ask him to buy one for her. Then she can make and mend the children's clothes, and this will be much more constructive than just accepting cash to pay for things that she may not really be able to afford in the long run.

In addition to the regular expenses, there are bound to be unexpected ones: the children have to subscribe to a leaving present for the form mistress at school; Mrs A has to go to the dentist, which involves a journey and possibly also the fee for treatment; the radio goes wrong and has to have a new valve. The first necessity after basic essentials have been looked after is a sort of marginal expense fund to cover the inevitable extras. If this proves impossible to achieve, then the whole picture must be reviewed again. Are there any more ways in which money could be raised? Could Mrs A get a better paid job, or cheaper accommodation for herself and the children? Could she let one room of the flat or pare down still further the weekly expenditure? It just is not realistic to expect to live on a fixed budget that allows nothing for incidental small expenses or mishaps. Mrs A may have a connection through her work or family with one of the organizations that has charitable funds available to help people in her position and is listed in the *Annual Charities Digest* probably available at your local library or Citizens' Advice Bureau. Her local Council also keeps a list of all charities in the area.

In doing her planning Mrs A will almost certainly find that advice from someone else will help. If she is not the sort of woman who is used to working this kind of thing out for herself, then maybe her brother, the people next door or someone at the local church may be willing to assist, or at least find someone who can. If she has a bank account, she could go and see the bank manager. Here is one of your greatest problems: asking other people for help means that you must admit to them that you have got into a mess and are having difficulty with managing. Such an admission is not easy to make, but look at it this way: if you once learn to cope then you will not need so much help in the future; you will be able to stand on your own feet, and in due time probably help someone else who is worse off than you are.

A certain amount of toughness develops, not because you want to be all that tough, but because the things that have happened to you have made you, in one way, stronger than you were before. But a tough person is not necessarily a 'hard' person, and the knowledge that you have coped with some problems is often the only assurance you have that you will be able to manage even bigger ones. Perhaps a local tradesman may be trying to overcharge you, and you have never liked to say anything about it. In fact, if you can bring yourself to dispute the figure he is asking you will find that later on you are agreeably surprised at yourself. There is no need to be worried if he turns surly or tries to sneer. Of course it is unpleasant, but this is the kind of behaviour that the less honest man is likely to adopt when he has been found out. You will find that he will be much less likely to try it again; he may not like you much, but he will respect you enough to know that you can stand up to him.

Managing money is not only a matter of working out a budget, which is really an estimate of what you expect to spend. It is also necessary to keep some kind of accounts. Lest some people be put off by this idea, we want to say that accounts can be very simple or fairly complicated, according to your needs and your skill. The most simple way is just to make a note of what you spend day by day, and add these items up at the end of each week and month. You can compare this with the budget you made previously, and it will help you to plan even better for the future. In even the most simple accounts it is possible to separate money spent on clothes from money used for rent, food, fares, fuel and so on. Accounts like this can be kept in an exercise book, and perhaps the greatest help they give is to reduce your worry.

Accounts do not of themselves produce more income, but they do help you to know where you are, which is very reassuring. Worry comes so often from wondering what is going to happen, from being unsure whether you are going to be able to manage.

One of the irritating things about being short of money is that one tends to think – and sometimes also talk – about it perpetually. This, like any other obsession, becomes a bore to oneself and everyone else. One way to cut down everlasting niggling is to fix an outside limit for the weekly grocery bill near where you think it should be. To keep within your limit, make the list before setting off to shop, starting with basic foods like fats, sugar, tea, and working up to things like cake and chocolate biscuits. Obviously you will take advantage of cheap offers where you can, but approach the thing from *your* angle and try to be positive about it. 'I need butter, margarine, lard, eggs, bacon, cereal and that is what I am going to bring home.' When you find that one kind of bacon offers you a free packet of lard you take that. You also take the cereal that has 2p. off instead of the one that is at its usual price. This leaves you a little extra for the nice but non-essential things which are specially good value if bought this week rather than next. But do not be 'conned' into buying cut-price things just because the packet says they are wonderful value.

It certainly helps to plan menus, to know what foods are in season and which cuts of meat are the cheaper ones. If you have never honestly bothered to find out these things, think about them now. Both television and radio give excellent, regular advice about food buying. Watch or listen to these programmes, even if there is no time to study books or pore over coloured charts which show, in great detail, the anatomy of an ox.

Keeping account of expenditure applies just as much, of course, to a man on his own as to a woman alone. Either of them may be able to put money aside, if they are fortunate, and it can be helpful to deposit this money with a Building Society, or in a Post Office or other savings account (see Chapter 3). If you keep a careful note of what this money is for, dividing, say, cash put aside for new clothes from that reserved for a summer holiday, you can keep another simple form of account, and let your money earn some interest at the same time. This is a rather more complicated way of putting money aside in time for different types of expenditure, but although it is more complicated it is also more profitable. To give an example, it might be possible, after saving steadily for a year, to have a savings account with a balance of £100, made up this way:

	£
Towards new suit	22·50
Gas and Electricity	5·40
Holiday Fund	34·25
Car Fund	26·70
Life Insurance	11·15
	£100·00

Clearly, looking at this total, we can see that a gas or electricity bill has recently been paid, as there is very little left in this particular fund. The money in the Car Fund is perhaps saved up for the annual tax payable soon, or maybe for a renewal of the annual insurance. Before long it should be possible to buy the new suit that is being saved for, and it also looks as if there is soon going to be enough money for quite a reasonable holiday.

Next, there is the problem of managing the house, flat or rooms where you are living. Whatever the temptations to let things go, it is very definitely worth keeping the place tidy and clean. Maybe you will not be able to improve the furniture, replace things as soon as you would wish, but your home can be made to look better rather than worse, and in addition this will mean that you will feel better about it. You have the satisfaction of knowing that you are doing your best with what you have got. And of course this applies just as much to a man as to a woman; even if friends do not expect a man to have had much practice in keeping a house or flat clean, he will have every right to be proud of being able to show that he can do it.

As we have said, being alone can make you very depressed, and this can lead to a casual attitude to housework, and to necessary repairs and decorating. If you have done your own decorating you will know that it is really not very difficult, nor very expensive. If you have lived in the place some time you may very well want to make changes. In some way these represent the fact you are making a new kind of life, putting a part of the past behind you. There is a definite boost to morale when you look at the room you have finished, and at the fresh paint on the staircase or in the hallway. There are good books on home decorating and on how to do the usual household repairs.

If you have no idea how to mend a fuse, clean a stained carpet, tighten loose screws, fix tiles, replace plaster, then do not hesitate to ask for help. Usually, people who know about these things are only too happy to air their superior knowledge and will really enjoy helping you. You are not imposing on their goodwill, and if you mention that you have this or that problem, they may offer their assistance. On the other hand one must face the fact that by some people your signs may be entirely misread. We mention this because so frequently divorced people of both sexes seem to experience it. The women who asks a friend's husband for help in thawing out her frozen pipes may find that the thawing out process goes far beyond what she intended or the pipes require. Probably you can deal with this, but in fact the involvement need not necessarily be sexual. Take, for instance, the man who initially offers to help with one job and then finds himself being incessantly called upon to do others. He has the difficult choice of allowing advantage to be taken of him, or of risking seeming unkind. Make sure that you do not put him in this position.

We have already said something about budgeting for holidays, but they need planning in other ways too. Naturally, you will be limited by the amount of money you have, but remember that it is thoroughly worth while to take a holiday if you can possibly manage it. It is not only a matter of taking a rest; in fact, quite a lot of holidays are not in the least restful. It is really the change, the opportunity to move to new surroundings, that is so beneficial. The first part of the planning concerns the time of year; holidays are less expensive in the spring and autumn than in the summer, so if you can take them at those times it will save you up to a quarter of the cost.

Arrangements may have to be made well in advance if several people are involved. In fact, if six friends are planning to go abroad together in June, the best time to start planning is the previous Christmas. This is, of course, the time when the travel agencies are producing their brochures for holidays at home and abroad, and as they are given away free there is a good deal of luxury to be had just looking through them, especially on a cold winter evening. You may prefer a holiday in Britain, by the seaside, but if you have never been abroad and wondered what it is like, you will find that many holidays overseas are cheaper than they are here. If you find the cost worrying, or you have saved up only a part of the money you need, you will find that for some tours you can make payments over a period of time. This is especially true for the main scheduled airlines. When booking a holiday you have to pay a deposit, and this will not be returned to you if you cancel. It is possible, though, to insure against the risk that injury or illness will prevent you from going, in which case your deposit will be returned.

For many people a holiday costing as much as £50 is a complete impossibility. This does not mean that you should give up trying. You might think of going to a holiday camp, which can be good value for money if you are on your own with children. Even a short outing, such as a coach ride to some place of interest, will be worthwhile. Some people exchange houses with friends in different areas; others go and stay with people who then return and are given hospitality. You might even consider a working holiday which would bring you in some money, if the work involved is something you quite enjoy doing, and could be combined with a visit to somewhere you would like to see. A change of ideas is what you are really after. The advertisement columns of *The Times, Sunday Times, Observer* or *The Lady* offer all sorts of possibilities. But, as ever, be careful to find out all details of exactly what is involved, so that you do not spend your holiday being overworked, underpaid and otherwise taken advantage of. If a holiday, or even a few days away, are not possible, then it is worth thinking in terms of a visit to the Zoo, a theatre, a football match. These events, though not very important in themselves, are proof that you are beginning to cope with life, and able to enjoy part of it in spite of the problems.

In managing everything from the weekly budget to the annual holiday, planning is worth while. It boosts your morale. Help can be got from friends, from books, and from your own increasing self-confidence. Managing life need not be a mountain of despair; it can become part of the way back to normal living.

CHAPTER 7

Helping Yourself

WE have talked in other chapters about getting help after divorce and separation, from the social services, from professional people, from organizations and individuals. What about helping yourself? In a sense you will have been doing this all along, each time you approach a stranger, write a letter, pick up the telephone in an effort to get your problems straightened out. To begin with, these efforts may be like distress signals – frantic cries for help, made sometimes in the right quarter, sometimes, as results show, definitely not. You are unhappy, frightened bewildered – perhaps desperate – hardly knowing what you are doing or what help you want, conscious only that you cannot cope alone.

Very many people, men as well as women, have felt like this. Indeed, you may never have felt so helpless before, so frequently in need of support from others. You may even feel ashamed and apologetic to be asking what seem to you so many favours that you see no possible chance of ever being able to return. Some days things will go right. You feel well, competent, cheerful. The first shock of being alone has begun to recede. Then, without warning, an illness puts you out of action or an accident lands you in the casualty department of a strange hospital, wondering who in the world you can call your next-of-kin. Or perhaps your pocket is picked of a few pounds, or your home burgled. And back you are right where you started, with the wolf at the door and panic round the next corner.

Be assured, if you have felt these things you are not alone. Nor are you hopeless, peculiar or weak. Everyone takes time to recover from shock – some longer than others – and to most people marriage break-up is a shock of devastating proportions. On the way to recovery there are bound to be setbacks. You may even have picked up this book during a setback, flipped through its pages and thought to yourself, 'That is all very well. These people do not understand. I cannot do these things they suggest, like writing letters and going to ministries and departments and offices. I have no time, the children are crying and I am too worn out to read, write, go, ask or think. All I can do is live from day to day wondering how long I can go on.' Agreed. There are times when all one can do is crawl about like a stunned animal, unable to attempt anything beyond the bare essentials. But in the nature of things – and of people – *this does not last for ever*. The instinct for survival is strong whether the danger be death from drowning or collapse from overwork. Eventually some form of rescue comes. Far from being bothered, the rescuer usually reacts by saying 'Why didn't you tell me before? If only we'd known, we'd have done something. Only too glad to help.' It is warm and heartfelt. You feel you can go on from there and start helping yourself. And you wonder why on earth you *did* struggle so long without saying anything.

The next stage, getting specialist help with legal problems, money and housing follows rather the same pattern. To begin with, you may be smothered under an avalanche of vast responsibility and never-ending small chores. Perhaps you put off tackling the business side of things which seems to you complicated and difficult. At length you manage to make a telephone call. The day is packed so tightly that thrusting your problem before a professional feels like driving a wedge into a solid wall. But you do it. And later you organise your work, the children or your thoughts, just for one afternoon so as to keep the appointment he gave you. It is a good idea to jot down beforehand the things you want his advice about. If you do not do this it may be such a relief to sit in a quiet room with an intelligent adult who listens to what you say, that you quite literally forget what you came about. After perhaps months spent tearing between exacting job and chaotic home, or passed exclusively in the company of silly-seeming children, it would be so good to talk to an adult about anything at all. But that is not the purpose of this visit. You have come to discuss your sleeplessness, or how to get maintenance money, or why your son is doing no work at school. You can have about half an hour, with luck, and then you will be expected to leave. Life seems suddenly reduced to two narrow channels – work and worry. Possibly such an interview will stir things up in your mind so that unexpectedly you want to cry. The whole experience knocks you off balance, and you return home with another kind of exhaustion and half your questions unanswered. However you may feel about it, something positive has been donc; progress had been made. Next time it will require less – even if only a fraction less – effort from you to take the initiative.

In the whole process of rehabilitation, progress is not likely to be equal on all fronts at once. For instance, the legal side of your story may be more or less resolved; you feel your affairs are in good hands, the date of the Hearing is fixed, trouble you foresaw about property or children has not materialised and the position looks good on the whole. On the other hand, money is still very uncertain, you have been encroaching on savings which shows you are really living beyond your means, and this obviously cannot go on indefinitely. Then, perhaps you are still living in the house that you had when he or she left you, and it is no longer suitable. Your job does not fit in with the children's school hours. In short, the legal position is clear, but what about everything else? It takes time and energy to think out adjustments and put them into practice. Curiously, perhaps, friends are often neither helpful nor understanding about this. It is surprising how many people will at once inquire of a man or woman left alone through death or divorce, 'I suppose you'll be moving now?' It does not seem to be widely realized that most people, if they lose one thing, cling extra tightly – anyhow for a while – to what is left. Nor is it understood that aloneness and independence do not arrive simultaneously. Independence, if it comes at all, has often to be worked out through a fairly painful struggle.

At the start of the struggle, it my be helpful to get clear in your mind where divorce has actually placed you. For some people, it is a means to an end, the way out of a marriage that felt bad into a new one that promises to be better. For others, the divorced state is more like a transit camp in which their stay may be long or short. It may even be permanent, but this, when it does happen, is something that comes about gradually. If you divorce without immediate plans for the future, you will probably find that certain things are built into the divorce situation and simply have to be accepted. The likelihood is that you will have less money, less comfort, security, companionship, sex, than you had – at least in theory – when you were married. It may still be possible for you to get some or all of these things, but probably at a new price. By this we do not simply mean that a divorced man may have to pay cash for sex. It is more difficult than that. The difficulty lies in discovering what you want most, and deciding what you are prepared to do without, or to put up with, in order to have it.

Looming large as ever are the big, familiar questions. Which does a woman put first, her job or her children? Should a woman marry a man she does not wholly like, but who loves her and offers her security? Does a man want a job that is exciting, but has odd hours and allows him little freedom, or one which though monotonous, is regular, secure and not too taxing? For people of both sexes, the conflict which these questions arouse is heightened after divorce. Probably you thought you had found the answers already, by marrying this or that man or woman, settling for such and such a job, having a certain number of children. Part of the bewilderment which divorce brings is caused by just this: you thought you had *made* all the basic decisions, that you had set the course of your life. And now, when you have incurred responsibility, lost freedom, used up a number of years, it suddenly seems that the answers you arrived at were wrong, the course you chose mistaken. Late, and with handicaps, you must begin one part of your life all over again. For some people this is dreadfully hard, but it is usually possible. Individuals vary so much, though, in their capacity to adjust and adapt, that it is simply not fair to yourself to say that because the so-and-so's had their affairs straightened out, and were happily remarried and doing nicely thank you, within a year, there must be something wrong if you cannot achieve the same.

One of your biggest changes is likely to be economic. Money which formerly supplied one household must now stretch to support two, or at any rate to cover two sets of living expenses. For a woman, this may mean that for the first time in her life, or after a period spent bringing up children, she must get a paid job in order to live. Or it may mean her taking a job that is better paid but less congenial than her present one. Jobwise, a man is likely to be affected rather differently. With a wife and/or children to support, as well as supporting himself under a different roof, probably the wisest thing he can do about his job is simply to stick to it. But in time even he may consider a change. The same kind of job with a different firm might offer more 'perks'; a similar job in another town might mean that travelling expenses could be cut; here too there might be some spare-time employment or further training available which would put up his earnings and occupy his lonely hours of so-called leisure. He may even alter his job completely. One man who had been a representative for a firm selling agricultural feeding-stuffs, after his wife left him to bring up two small children, accepted his brother's suggestion that he should join forces with him in a flourishing landscape gardening business. The change virtually meant self-employment, involved hardly any long-distance travelling and gave the children the added security of an aunt and uncle close at hand.

Beware of the temptation to throw a good job over just because of the stress you have been through. It is all too easy to want to put all the past out of your mind, and to think that you can do this simply by moving away and by changing jobs. Quite the reverse may be true. If you abandon a good job at a time when you really need a solid base, this could turn out to be something you will very much regret. And if you are thinking that people will talk about you behind your back at work, well, they will, but not for ever. Your problems will of course be of interest to them, and this may not be easy to take, but the trouble will pass, as it always does, and you may then be very glad that you kept the job after all.

What about jobs for women? If you already have a good job, you may feel that it is your best anchor in the sea of uncertainty that divorce has flooded round you. You make your job the constant factor, and plan other things round it. Or, if you have good qualifications, they may be the first lead that you follow, even if you also have children to look after. A graduate who parted from her husband, found herself with no home, no money and two babies. Reckoning her degree to be the biggest asset she had, she first used that to get herself a well-paid job, then found a house she could rent out of her salary and lastly engaged a girl to look after the children while she was out earning. The same woman could have chosen to live entirely off the State and do no work outside her home. She chose instead to be self-supporting, a course which at times proved extremely hard, especially at the beginning – but nevertheless right for *her*. If you have not worked since the days before your marriage, and now feel inadequate for anything and everything, you might begin by asking yourself quite simply what, as a person, you have to offer. What, if anything, are you qualified to do? What do you enjoy doing? What are you good at? Pause over these two questions. If there is something you enjoy doing and other people find difficult or boring, you have a basis for a job. All sorts of personal services exist nowadays which are the result of a bright idea backed by some business sense – and this is not uncommon in women. Where does your particular ability lie? Are you good with children, animals, machines, figures, people? Can you cook, sew, type, write shorthand, drive a car? List on a piece of paper, everything you can do and waste no time thinking about what you cannot. The sight of so much positive information about yourself ought to hearten you. *Of course* you are worth employing.

The sort of job you go for may depend more on the time you have available and the amount of money you need than on any qualifications or training you may have. To take an extreme example, one divorced mother with a degree in archaeology took temporary work as a cleaner because this was the only job she could find nearby and with hours that fitted in with the needs of her children.

Much will depend on the area where you live and the work that is available locally. Then, how will you get to and from work? How much will this cost and how long will it take? If your children are not yet at school, is there a day nursery near where you live, and will places be available there for the children? There is a countrywide shortage of day nurseries and day nursery places, so it is as well to make certain about this. Most vital, also, who will look after the children if and when they are ill?

If you can look at the facts clearly and answer these questions, particularly the last one – for yourself – it will save a lot of time and disappointment. Some mothers answer many advertisements and apply for numerous posts only to face repeated rejection; employers foresee absence from work when the children are ill, and prefer to take another applicant who can be single-minded about the job. Put yourself in the position of the employer and you cannot fail to see his point of view, hard though it may seem to you. If you are thinking of working full-time, with perhaps three weeks' holiday a year, have you thought of what will happen to the children in the holidays, or at week-ends when you have to do shopping and catch up with housework? Will they be unsupervised all or much of the time, and have you thought of possible consequences? Unless you have a really good arrangement to cover holidays and emergencies you might be wise to reconsider the whole position. After poverty, the divorced mother's worst nightmare is illness in herself or her children. Less vivid in her imagination, but often present, is the fear that the children may become delinquent or out of hand. Are you honestly in a position to hold down a regular job and give your children the time and attention you want to give them, or should you be looking for something rather different? Some jobs offer accommodation. For instance, if you have one small child, it might be wise to consider taking a job as a housekeeper or mother's help at least until your child is a little older. Advertisements for these posts often say that a child would be welcome.

If you have children of school age, you might think of a job in a school, where your own children could be educated. Work in a school, whether teaching or non-teaching, still seems one of the best solutions for the woman with school-age children of her own. If teaching appeals to you, but you have no previous training, it may be possible for you to take a teacher training course. Most training colleges take mature students now, and you should apply to your Local Education Authority for details. The Department of Education and Science, Curzon Street, London, W.1, publishes booklets called Grants to Students, which give details of financial help for which you may qualify. Perhaps teaching is not for you, but the idea of doing some study or training that will stand you in good stead later on is well worth considering, if your financial state will allow. The Advisory Centre for Education (ACE Ltd), 32 Trumpington Street, Cambridge, will provide a book-list on request, as well as a fund of information on all aspects of adult education. Part-time day and evening classes are held in all kinds of domestic and academic subjects as well as office skills. Enquiries about courses available in your area can be made to the Local Education Authority; each course will cost you around £5 per year. There is also the Open University which offers an opportunity for adults throughout the country to study for degree qualifications through the media of integrated television, radio and specially designed correspondence courses. Those who wish to apply for details should write to Admissions Office, The Open University, P.O. Box 48, Bletchley, Bucks.

If you can plan the rest of your time-table to allow for it, a course of study with or without an examination at the end of it might help you to get a better paid or more interesting job later on when commitments are less binding. If you already have a job with a firm or are thinking of working part-time in a shop or store, make inquiries: many firms will pay for their employees to take further training – shorthand and typing for instance, or retail management – provided the employee signs on with them for a definite period after the end of training.

There are also correspondence courses. For anyone who suffers from being alone, the idea of a correspondence course may not be attractive. On the other hand, in certain circumstances this kind of instruction, which can help you towards new qualifications or enable you to make money at home, may be a worthwhile stop-gap. Mrs C, living in the country and with four children at home, was hardly in a position to take an outside job. She had no room in her cottage to take a paying-guest, and very little spare time left when she had finished seeing to house, garden and children. More as an amusement for winter evenings than with much thought of making money, she enrolled with a school of journalism which advertised in one of the Sunday papers. She found the course interesting and stimulating, and before she was half-way through had earned a number of useful cheques and made some good contacts for the future.

The great thing, if you are thinking of a correspondence course, is to ascertain, before you enrol, how long you are allowed for each batch of work. It is no use enrolling on a course which demands more work than you are capable of doing in a given time. Some courses have no rules about time. Others have strict ones, so it is vital to check this before you start. The schools which run these courses produce attractive brochures, and hold out gleaming hopes of a big income. Try to ignore the exaggeration of their sales-talk and look instead of the reality of the offer and its value to you. Remember that the schools make much of their profit out of people who do not finish their courses. Discuss it with a friend before you commit yourself, and sleep on the idea once or twice before you pay the school any money. Ensure that the school with which you enrol has been accredited with the Department of Education and Science.

It could be said of all work undertaken by divorced women with dependent children: do try not to take on more than you can manage. Your own health and your children's welfare come first. Money comes into it obviously, but try to let your decision about a job depend more on what money you *need* than on what money you think it would be nice to have. And remember that even a job which sounds well-paid often proves not to be so profitable if one adds up the cost of all that it means in the way of fares, hair-do's, clothes, time-saving foods, help with house or children.

If you are looking for a job near where you are living – more or less anything that will bring in a wage – you can either visit an employment agency, answer likely advertisements in a local paper, or go to the Labour Exchange. If you are looking for a residential job and are prepared to live in another area, then the national newspapers – *The Times, Daily Telegraph,* the *Guardian* and *The Lady* (weekly) – offer a wide assortment. For school jobs, the *Times Educational Supplement* (weekly) has advertisements for all jobs connected with schools. Other sources of information are the Local Education Authority, and for fee-paying schools the educational consultants Gabbitas, Thring of 6 Sackville Street, London W.1. and Truman and Knightley of 93 Baker Street, London W. 1.

So far we have talked about paid jobs – work that fits in with your family commitments, uses your particular abilities and earns you a living. For some women with young children it is either impossible, uneconomic or undesirable to have a paid job. There may be no absolute need for them to work: in some circumstances it could be best that a woman should draw supplementary benefit and stay at home looking after the children. Or maybe her maintenance payment will be sufficient to live on. In some ways this woman is much better off than the one who told us, 'I had no time to think about how I felt; I had no money at all, I didn't know where the next meal was coming from, and I just had to work for it.' She was looking back ten years to the time when she was first alone. Yet hard though her life had been, she thought that in some ways she had been better off than the woman not forced by necessity to go out of her home, make fresh contacts, plunge into a job.

If you come into the category of those who do not have to work, it may require considerable effort from you to go and find out about a voluntary job. But this is a way of helping yourself out of loneliness towards independence, and we strongly recommend it. There are innumerable agencies which depend largely on volunteer workers, and your local Public Library or Citizens' Advice Bureau will have a list of these and information about local branches. Again it will be necessary to find work that fits in with other commitments and uses what time and talent you have to offer. A non-working mother of children under five might involve herself and her children with a playgroup, or even start one if none exists already locally. Information about playgroups and how to run them can be obtained from the Pre-School Playgroups Association of 87a Borough High Street, London S.E.1.

Besides work, another big decision you may have to make will be between staying in the area where you have lived while married, and moving away from it to begin your 'new' life in a new place. Of course this may be decided for you by circumstances. If you are the partner who leaves, then where to go may well have been one of your first problems. Often, though, there is an interim stage before any long-term living arrangements are made, so you may have time to consider where you are going to live. For some, moving may sound attractive, and phrases like 'clean break', 'fresh start' and 'new ground' have an inviting ring about them. Others, to whom a particular home may mean security, will make that the constant factor and plan on from there. If you are thinking of moving, remember that it is expensive, and that all sorts of time-consuming things go with it, like finding your way around, discovering new shops and services, new doctor and dentist, new schools and new acquaintances who will only become friends when still more time has been spent on getting to know them. It is not always easy to sort out priorities; you may see pros and cons flickering round every issue and find it exceedingly difficult to assess the position realistically. Every advantage seems to be offset by its own snag and every hope will have built-in fears. It may be helpful to write down your problem. 'Am I going to leave the place where I have lived for six years or am I going to stay?' Divide your sheet of paper into two columns and write Fors on one side and Againsts on the other. Bear in mind that friends and contacts (the little man round the corner who can make this or mend that for *half* the price) can make a tremendous difference to life if one is living it alone and on a shoestring. If you have children, think of their feelings too. Remember that there will be friends of their age as well as friends of yours who may be able to do quite a lot to give them a sense of security. If you are ill or have to leave them even temporarily for some reason, the neighbour they have known all their lives will be far more reassuring to them than a neighbour from any new house next door. If the children are of school age, find out about schools in the other area.

This is the kind of situation which could arise; Mrs D, after her divorce, planned to go and live near her parents in another part of the country. Her principal aim was to get back to work at full-time nursing for which she was qualified, and she thought that this would be easier with her mother on hand to help. Her younger child, a daughter, was only seven and could have changed school without much upset. However, her elder son had just started and was doing well at the new local comprehensive school, an impressive building splendidly equipped. Education where her parents lived was going through a difficult transition stage. Comprehensive schools were on the way, but the most likely school for her son at the moment would be a secondary modern housed in out-of-date buildings. After investigation, Mrs D decided to remain in the same county and tried to solve her own employment problem locally rather than risk upsetting her son's education or holding back his development.

Through a friend, Mrs D heard of a job which, although it did not make direct use of her nursing qualifications, offered certain advantages. A husband and wife, each of whom had a career, wanted a housekeeper-mother's help to look after two small boys at day-school. They offered a rent-free flat in their large house, plus a small wage and a degree of freedom which no hospital job could possibly have allowed. There would be just room for Mrs D's children in the flat, and the employers made no objection to them. On a balance-sheet of the kind we suggested, Mrs D's problem might look something like this:

Problem: Whether or not to move.

for	*against*
Good use could be made of Mrs D's qualification.	Loss of good school for son.
Nearness to good hospital.	Shortcoming of new school.
Interesting job.	Loss of friends for Mrs D and the children.
Support of parents.	Expense of moving.
Change of scene. New friends.	

Problem: Whether to take job offered.

for	*against*
Free accommodation.	Low wages.

for	*against*
Son could stay at present school.	If job proves unsatisfactory, giving notice means loss of home.
Reasonable freedom.	Dull work.
Security in having a family at hand.	Irregular hours.
A man in the background for son.	Mrs D may feel more lonely alongside a married couple.

The last items in each column are really unknowns. These simply cannot be judged until the thing is tried. Whether or not Mrs D works efficiently, success or failure in this job will depend finally on her ability to get on with her employers. If at first things do not go well, Mrs D would be wise not to give up too soon. She will have had many doubts about the decision, and any little – or big – problem may sway her feelings unduly. It will be worth her while to stick to her decision for a reasonable time, and to give the job a fair try.

This brings us to the whole question of relationships. There is no doubt that most people who divorce find that in all sorts of ways it affects their attitude towards other people and other people's attitude towards them. If you look back you will probably remember that, although it was a different kind of change, something of the same sort happened when you married. Marriage, as well as bringing you a share of your husband's or wife's friends, was also a pass ticket to social gatherings of other married couples. Gradually you tended to lose touch socially with your contemporaries who were not married. And if you had children, another change probably came when they arrived. You saw less of childless friends but met more people through the children. Each change in circumstances brings a change in relationships, but divorce often brings loss without any obvious compensating gain. To take a simple example: a man and his wife, both very keen ballroom dancers, used often to go out dancing with other married couples in the provincial town in the north of England where they lived. The husband danced very well and was a popular partner. After his wife left him, he found that other husbands no longer liked their wives to dance with him and found excuses to prevent it. Hard treatment to take when he already felt rejected by his wife. Attitudes towards divorce and divorced people vary very much in different parts of the country as well as in different sections of society. On the other hand it would be wrong to suppose that attitudes are always determined by anything as impersonal as geography, tradition or even religious principles. People's unexpected and sometimes unsympathetic reactions to friends who divorce are often caused by a sort of fear. It may be fear of having to divide loyalty between a divorcing husband and wife, both of whom are close friends; it may be fear that if this happened to *them* it could also happen to *us* – the idea that divorce is in some way 'catching'. It may be a personal doubt. 'We always liked Richard so much. We thought we knew him well. Now he's left Jane, we don't know what to think.' Doubt may also spread to Jane. Like this: 'He wouldn't have left her without some reason. Perhaps we were wrong about her.' It may be a fear of saying the wrong thing, the wish not to be mixed up in anything 'unpleasant'. Or it may be the most straightforward fear of all. Richard and/or Jane will be looking for a new partner. 'One of them might break up our marriage.'

Risk. It is real and there is no point at all in pretending it does not exist, both for the married and for the divorced. Think of Mrs D, whom we mentioned earlier, and whose problems seemed so happily solved when she heard of a job that offered her a home, a wage and a share in the life of another family. This kind of arrangement *could* work. Equally, things could go wrong. A lonely woman whose own marriage has recently broken up, might well come to feel resentment towards a happily married couple of whom she saw a great deal. If their marriage was less happy or going through a difficult patch, having her around might make it much worse or even wreck it completely. Before long Mrs D could cease to look like the Deserted Wife and begin to resemble the Other Woman. So soon after her divorce she would be particularly vulnerable emotionally. Yet here was a good job, which for economic and practical reasons sounded a good proposition despite the built-in emotional risk. If both sides were aware of the kind of feelings that could develop they would be forearmed, and this would go a long way towards making the thing a success.

The same sort of difficulties could arise in an office where a divorcee falls in love with a married boss or vice versa. Or it could be another emotion: one divorcee had to give up her job and find another, because the first boss reminded her so much of her ex-husband that she could not bear to work for him. Some people form good relationships easily and quickly, others do not. After divorce, even the former group may be lonely, because as we have said friends and relations sometimes behave oddly and opportunities for meeting new people are few. The fewer relationships there are, the more important they become. When you are newly divorced and lonely, vulnerable and over-busy, what practical steps can you take that will help you towards re-establishing relationships with other people?

One way of checking on how you are coping is by seeing how other people act in a similar situation. When you are divorced this is not always easy. You possibly know a few divorced people, but their way of life is quite different from yours, and perhaps it has never struck you that you have much in common. But circumstances alter things; two lone parents attending a function at their children's school are naturally drawn together. The less shy of the two asks if anyone is sitting in this seat, and feelers start tentatively waving between them. (Is this someone who understands? Someone like me?) It is heartening to discover that one is not alone in being alone. But occasions when this kind of thing happens are not all that frequent, and some people are too shy to take advantage of them when they do. If divorced people like meeting other divorced people, why not start an organization to bring them together?

Briefly, this was the idea behind the first Divorced and Separated Clubs, which began forming in this country some years ago. There were starts and false starts. Often, the most lively members, having met at the club, married and were then too occupied to come to it. Then it is easy to see how unscrupulous promoters could take advantage of people in the divorce situation to create a sort of Re-marriage Bureau – expensive, exclusive and of doubtful standards. People were suspicious of the whole idea. Clubs were formed and faded away. Then, in 1966, ten existing independent clubs in and around London joined together to form the National Federation of Clubs for the Divorced and Separated. Under their auspices, affiliated clubs were set up all over the country, wherever local people were ready to start them, and there are now over fifty of these. As yet the Federation is not a strong body, because it has naturally been difficult to collect funds. In the United States, there are many similar clubs, usually called Parents Without Partners and, as they have now built up a big and popular organization there, it seems likely that in time to come the Federation will enlarge its influence in this country.

How do the clubs work and what sort of people will you meet there? Mr E and Mrs F first met at one of these clubs. It was called the Phoenix Club locally, a title which symbolized the beginning of a return to normal life of people who were formerly married. Mr E joined the club before Mrs F, a whole year before. He saw an advertisement in the local paper advertising a coffee evening, and only went along because he had nothing else to do. He expected to see some old ladies handing out coffee, but when he found the building where the club was meeting that night he was greeted by a young woman of his own age who said, 'Go straight up and find yourself a seat – if there are any left.' He went up some stairs and into a large room where there were about thirty people of various ages sitting around, some on the floor, others in chairs, noisily chatting and laughing. There were rather more women than men, and he found himself talking to a cheerful, plump girl, who turned out to be the Club Secretary. Making a contribution of only fifteen pence towards coffee and refreshments, he had a very good evening, and determined to come back again.

Mr E enjoyed company, and before long was fully involved in the affairs of the club. He was rather surprised to find that there were a lot of club activities. A typical month's programme would include:

A coach trip to the coast for parents and children.
A regular weekly visit to a nearby pub where the beer was good.
A jazz record group and also (less crowded) a classical music group.
Two dances in his own area, with invitations to others at neighbouring Phoenix Clubs.
Coffee evenings, like the one he first attended.
Bottle parties.
One rather serious discussion group, which tended mostly to deal with personal problems and difficulties. This did not much appeal to Mr E, but it seemed to be well attended, for the discussion was led fortnightly by a local social worker.
A monthly visit to a local theatre where block booking enabled members to get seats at a reduced price.
Committee meetings.
A jumble sale to raise cash for the coming Christmas party for children.

This was, of course, not all that the club provided. A good deal was done by the members for one another. One girl, for instance, appeared at a coffee evening, looking tired, worried and run down. She left, having hardly spoken a word, but the Secretary later made discreet inquiries and found that she and her baby daughter were living temporarily with relatives and would shortly be homeless. She had very little money and was at her wits' end to know what to do. Another committee member knew of a living-in job that offered a small basement flat. Various members had bits of furniture they were not using. By their united efforts the club managed to provide all that one woman needed to start a new life. Then, members helped one another with decorating or moving house, baby-sitting or transport. Some people came to the club pretty regularly; some came once or twice and never again; and, of course, some made close friendships with other members.

To start with, Mr E spent most of the time talking to other men about the problem of cooking and housework, of coping with maintenance payments and seeing the children. Then he began to go out – diffidently at first – with some of the women members of the club. Over the next year he got to know two of them well, and had a brief affair with each. This did not leave him very satisfied and the relationships did not develop any further. Then Mrs F joined the club. She became a member at the suggestion of a friend and her first visit was to a children's party where she took her two small sons. Later, she used to go to coffee evenings and there she met Mr E, who started to take her out regularly. They soon got to know one another very well and spent several nights together. This was rather unsatisfactory for both of them, because it involved cold early morning trips back home for Mr E, using his motor-bike. Eventually they agreed that he should move into her house, paying part of the rent. This worked well, her children liked him and after a time they got married.

We do not want to paint so rosy a picture that you will expect a Divorced and Separated Club to solve all your problems. Clubs vary according to locality, number of members, social facilities available, and apart from these things can have some disadvantages. Mrs G joined a club about three months after her divorce. She had been deserted by her husband only eighteen months after their marriage, and he had gone off with a younger girl. Going back to live with her parents, she could scarcely face the world at all, but eventually she heard about the local club and plucked up courage to go along. On the second evening she met Mr H, a pleasant young man who liked her and paid her a lot of attention, the one thing she needed more than anything else. He took her out, gave her small presents, and wanted to make love to her. At first she was shocked, because her husband had been the only man with whom she had had intercourse, but as she thought more about it she decided she was being silly, and she went to bed with him several times. He was more considerate than her husband, and she soon fell in love with him. Mr H was not by any means unkind but, although he liked Mrs G and enjoyed going to bed with her, he had no intention at all of making a permanent relationship. He was quite used to having intercourse with girls and, as he was an attractive man, he was able to take his pick. This he did, not thinking much about the effect it would have on them. After some time he started to go out with another girl from the club (one who incidentally took him a good deal less seriously than Mrs

G, which he found a distinct relief). He did not give Mrs G up altogether, but only saw her once a fortnight or so. When she found out about the other girl, she broke down completely and was in an even worst state than she had been following her divorce. For her this was the second rejection in six months, a final proof that she was no use to anyone, could neither attract nor hold any man permanently and she became shut off and very depressed. Her doctor helped her with pills, but she only took them irregularly and spent two spells in a mental hospital. After one of these she took an overdose of her pills, and died alone in her parents' home one night when they had gone out to see some friends.

This happened. It is a most extreme and disastrous example but it shows how a person can come to believe that they are worthless, not because someone tells them so, but simply because they pass again through the same bitter experience within a short time. Possibly, if Mrs G had led a fuller life and could have been really interested in things – a job, a hobby, events that went on in the town where she lived, she would not have chosen to die. If she had known more people, among them someone who could have helped her to see what she, as a person, had to offer, the affair with Mr H would not have been so tragically vital to her life.

News of her death came as a great shock to many other members of the club, who felt that surely they could somehow have prevented it. But could they? Mrs G's story illustrates another difficulty that can arise – not only in clubs of course, but here the fact that everyone is 'unattached' makes it all the more likely. Several of the members – of both sexes – will think nothing of casual sexual intercourse, and in fact this will have become their expectation after spending an evening with one another. We discuss this in more detail in Chapter 11, but you should know before you join a club that although there will be all sorts of club socials and activities, it may be that from time to time some sexual pressure is put on you by individual members, and you should if possible have some idea in mind of how you intend to react to it. For the shy person just emerging from the shadow of their own divorce, an assumption that intercourse will take place between a man and a woman who have spent one or two evenings together can be very distressing.

A great many members of Divorced and Separated Clubs join them because they are hoping to find someone else and to marry again. Other people say they join for the opposite reason; badly hurt by the break-up of one marriage, they have no wish either to be picked up or paired off. But they do want companionship. At their best, the clubs help people to start regaining the confidence they have lost. They may well have forgotten the art of building bridges to other people, and have become isolated on their own islands of misery. The clubs can sometimes help them to start rebuilding these bridges to one another, and this can lead to their being able to return to society, to meet and talk to people at work, and get back to a full social life. In addition, the busy programmes of many of the clubs and the opportunity to help organize these, keeps many of the members from relapsing into a life of sad loneliness, gazing every night at their television sets. Also, the fact that you are among a lot of other people, some of whom may well be in a worse position than you are, will keep you from becoming too sorry for yourself. Not only this, but there will be other people who have been through the same trouble that now burdens you, and may be able to tell you how they managed. It is also healthy to be with a group of people who do not waste too much time being sorry for one another, but try instead to make the most of what they have.

One danger of these clubs – which non-joiners are quick to point out – is that they can become inward-looking, so that members do not have much contact with people who are not members. You belong just as much to the rest of the world as you do to the club, and there is nothing to restrain you from seeking and making relationships outside it. Indeed, you will succeed in leading a more balanced life if you do. It is a mistake to think that the rest of society has nothing to offer, even if you do from time to time have unfortunate experiences, and people seem to treat you as a different kind of person once they know you are divorced. Club members can sometimes become so inward-looking that, feeling the world has rejected them, they are unwilling to look outside their own circle for help and friendship.

If there is no club near where you live, you might start one of your own. The National Federation has a useful set of descriptive leaflets which will help you to form a club, and one of their officers may even be able to visit your area and help with the initial stages. There are not many formalities; you and one or two others can in fact create the kind of club that suits you best. There is a very small affiliation fee paid to the Federation, and each club is free to make its own financial arrangements. Subscriptions are kept as low as possible. Federated clubs have to be geared to the financial difficulties which most of their members are facing.

Helping yourself, however you set about it, takes energy – mental and physical. Apart from laziness, the things which make you least capable of helping yourself are being ill, overtired or under-nourished. Take what steps you can to prevent these things or to put them right, and you will be giving yourself a fair chance of success.

CHAPTER 8

The Children

WHAT happens to the children of people who divorce? A huge question, but since divorce is a legal operation, perhaps we should start by considering how the law attempts to answer it. First, the decree will not legally be made absolute until arrangements for the care and upbringing of children under sixteen 'have been made and are satisfactory or are the best that can be devised in the circumstances'. Secondly, and this narrows down the issue still further, it must be decided what is satisfactory and it must sometimes be decided which is best of several possible solutions.

In the whole drama of divorce, facts and feelings are nowhere more uncertain or more dangerously confused than as they concern the children. For them, the divorce of their parents may be better than living in a home full of hostility and discord. But often this is arguable, and in any case their well-being is still going to be very much affected by what happens *after* the divorce. Where will they live, and with whom? How much will they see of the absent parent, and where will they fit into the second marriages their parents may make or second families of which they are suddenly a part?

No parent can look dispassionately at his or her own child, and it is recognized that in this situation, where passions run high, children would be at risk if their future were left entirely in the hands of their parents. British law, therefore, in granting two people a divorce, makes arrangements for the welfare of their children the concern of the Court which hears the case. Even after the decree is made absolute, either parent may, through solicitors or on their own, appeal to the Court in any dispute concerning the children. In certain circumstances, when the children leave the country and go abroad, for instance, formal application must be made to the Court. This is quite a simple procedure but it illustrates the rather special relationship which continues to exist between the Court, an authority which is neither prying nor punitive, and those children whose parents' marriage it once dissolved.

There is bound to be an interval of time – six months or more – between the parents' separation and the Court Hearing. During this time the children have to live with someone – their mother or father, friends, relatives or, where no other arrangements can be made, they may have to be put in the care of the Local Authority. In the divorce petition itself, the petitioner has to make proposals about the future of any children under the age of sixteen, and at the Hearing questions are asked about these proposals. It may be that existing arrangements seem satisfactory, acceptable to both parents and adequate in the opinion of the Judge. Suppose, for instance, that a petition is brought by a mother who has her two children living with her. She does not go out to work, has suitable accommodation, and the maintenance payment from her husband is sufficient to support them; her husband does not dispute her plea for custody of the children, but merely asks that he may have reasonable access to them. There is nothing about the mother which suggests that she is not a fit person to be in charge of the children. A few brief questions are asked of her when she is in the witness-box, and that is all. If, on the other hand, a father is petitioning, if he has children whom he looks after single-handed besides doing a job away from home, and if he is asking for custody of them, investigations are likely to be far more searching before the Judge is satisfied. Are the children being properly looked after, properly fed, clothed and cared for? What happens if they are ill? Possibly the father has a record of instability, or it may be alleged that he drinks heavily at times. Even without these characteristics, a man on his own is not readily granted custody of a young family.

Other factors could give a Judge cause for concern. There may be a history of ill-health or of mental instability in the parent with whom the children are living. There may be bad housing, overcrowding, lack of adequate supervision because the parent in charge is out at work. The children may be separated from one another, staying temporarily with relatives, or may have come before the Juvenile Court. It may have been proposed that a child should accompany one parent who intends to emigrate after the divorce, to marry and live abroad or to return to his or her country of origin. There may be special difficulty if one child in a family is backward, handicapped, or particularly dependent emotionally on the absent parent. Custody by one parent may be contested by the other. Access may be unreasonably denied, wisely prevented or dangerously abused. A Judge, if he is not satisfied by what he is told in the petition and at the Hearing, may adjourn the case so as to give time for further inquiries to be made.

The person who conducts this inquiry is the Divorce Court Welfare Officer, who will visit the home where the children are living and will interview both parents. If they live in different parts of the country, Welfare Officers from the two areas may carry out the interviews and contribute this section of the report. The Officer in charge of the case will meet and talk to the children as well as interviewing any prospective step-parent. He can, if he wishes, extend his inquiries to the family doctor, school teacher, or any other appropriate 'person of standing' whose observations could be helpful. Great care goes into the making of the Welfare Officer's report. It is seen by the children's parents as well as by their legal representatives, and the Officer must be prepared to substantiate what it states – possibly under cross-examination. He has access to court files for information on the case, but more important in the report are his own impressions and observations.

A great deal of effort is spent in trying to establish the truth about a difficult case, the sole aim being the welfare of the children. Occasionally a Judge will even interview the children himself. When he has sufficient information to form an opinion, he will give the Court's decision on who shall have custody. Custody means ultimate responsibility, and may be awarded to either mother or father or to both jointly if such a solution seems practicable. Where a father is awarded custody and the children are actually living with their mother, she is given what is called 'care and control', which means that she looks after the children's everyday needs, but important issues such as those affecting education, religion and marriage are the responsibility of the father. On the whole, the Court prefers that children wherever possible – particularly those under seven years old – live with their mother; and it is a general principle that children of one family should not be split up.

If, as occasionally happens, there are what the law calls 'exceptional circumstances' and the Judge thinks it is in a child's best interest to be in the care of someone other than the parents, he may make a 'Supervision Order'. This means that the child, though living perhaps with a relative or friend, is under the supervision of the Local Authority, in the person of Welfare Officer, or Child Care Officer, who visits regularly and generally keeps an eye on the child.

There are several statutory services and individuals who are concerned with the young, namely the Child Care Service, Child Guidance Clinics, Probation Officers, Youth Employment Officers and Education Welfare Officers. It is possible that a child who has been through some kind of family disaster will show signs of distress in difficult behaviour, even violence. Experience shows that, even when this does happen, children normally pass through this phase and do not return to it, but of course it is very worrying while it is going on. If your child is behaving in a way that you cannot control and that worries you seriously, go and see the Child Care Officer of your Local Authority.

The Child Care Service is run by the Children's Department of the county or county borough council; it has been in existence only a little over twenty years, and at first dealt only with children who had to be 'taken into care' of the local Council. It still does this work, finding homes for children who are temporarily or permanently without someone to look after them. An increasing amount of the work of the Child Care Officers, however, is now with families which have not broken up, but which threaten to do so. They therefore see many mothers who are coping alone with their children, and from time to time are also involved helping with marital problems as well. In charge of the Child Care Officers, who visit homes and see parents and children, is the Children's Officer, whose office is at the Children's Department locally, and whom you can usually see if you want. Normally, though, your request for help will be met by a visit from a Child Care Officer, who is very used to dealing with all kinds of problems affecting young people under the age of seventeen. In one day he may be helping an unmarried mother, a family threatened with eviction, and a teenager caught driving away a car not belonging to him.

A child who is deeply disturbed may best be helped at a Child Guidance Clinic. These Clinics also help young people who are educationally retarded, and may also be able to see that they are given a more suitable type of education than they are now having. Clinics do not exist in every area, but they have in charge a psychiatrist. Also available are a psychologist and a social worker. These three people are able to deal with most of the severe problems of the young, and referral to the Clinic is usually made by a doctor or schoolteacher rather than direct by the parent. So if you feel that this is the sort of help that you and your child need, see your own doctor about it, the schoolmaster or the Education Welfare Officer. This skilled help is given not only to the child, but also to the parent.

If you go to a Child Guidance Clinic, expect to see the psychiatrist for an interview, and also be prepared for your son or daughter to have various tests. These tests, the interview with the parent, and reports from the doctor and the school, are all factors that the Clinic takes into account before recommending a course of action to you. This may be that there should be an alteration in your child's present school programme, a transfer to another school, or some other step, depending on his needs, and also on the facilities that are within reach of where you live. Children are only very rarely parted from the parent, a course of action only suitable in extreme cases.

We mentioned the Education Welfare Officer, who may refer the child to the Clinic. If he needs to go to a special school, this Officer will also make all the necessary arrangements, and will keep in touch with the parent. He can also be a great help if you have some kind of problem that you do not, for various reasons, want to discuss with your child's headmaster. You can find the Education Welfare Officer at the local Education Office. If in difficulty, ask your local Council for the address, and write there first for an appointment if a visit would involve a long journey.

By no means all children have serious emotional problems, but many may be puzzled what job to take up when they leave school. Where a mother is on her own with her child, she may find it very difficult to know what job is best. Youth Employment Officers visit schools and help young people who have not yet settled on the type of job they want. They also see the parent, or parent and child together, at their office. This by no means only applies where a boy or girl is looking for their first job. Quite often you will find that the first job does not attract your son or daughter, who say they want something completely different. Many young people feel this way. It can be a sign that they are finding it difficult to settle to anything, but it can also mean that they simply have come to dislike their first – or second – job, and need help to find the right one. Your local Council, the Labour Exchange, the Citizens' Advice Bureau, or of course the school where your child is, can give you the Youth Employment Officer's address. (There is an excellent publication *Careers For Girls* mentioned in our book list, p. 193.)

From what we have said it will be obvious that extensive machinery has been devised by the Welfare State to look after the interests of all children, and that this is especially valuable to children whose parents are separated or divorced. There is a general awareness that divorce creates problems for children, but of course there are limits to what legal and social machinery can do about helping to solve them. For one thing, at the time of the divorce no one can foresee the shape or the severity of these problems, or where they are going to arise. Nor does anyone know how the two parents are going to fare after they separate, although this will greatly affect the children. Take the mother we mentioned earlier, whose case appeared to be so straightforward, and who was granted custody of her two children with the minimum of questions asked: Mrs H's children were aged seven and four when her husband left home. Mrs H was the obvious person to bring up the children. She was their mother and though an undemonstrative girl, she genuinely loved and wanted them, and they her. So the judgement was unquestionably a right one, not only in principle but also in practice at the time it was made. What happened afterwards?

Mrs H, shy by nature and shattered by her husband having left her, went out very little after her divorce, engrossing herself with her home and children, When they were a little older and both at school all day she took a secretarial job in another school locally. The work was dull, but the holidays fitted in with the children's. She made a number of new acquaintances at work and among the parents of the children's schoolfriends, but her social life was very restricted. She had one love affair which, though passionate while it lasted, left her feeling so hurt and the children so unsettled that she afterwards became even more enclosed than before. Gradually, in spite of having the children with her, Mrs H grew chronically lonely, and her intense absorption in their lives irritated them increasingly, especially the daughter.

Mr H's story following the divorce was very different. After a time he remarried, started a second family and, having previously found it difficult to see his son and daughter, now wanted them to go and stay regularly with him. Reluctantly, Mrs H allowed brief visits. Both children, after a cautious start, thoroughly enjoyed getting to know their young stepmother who was a warm, sympathetic person and liked having them. They in no way thought of her as a replacement for their mother; they just liked her for herself. And they liked the experience of being elder brother and sister to their two small half-brothers. They also began really to know their father. When he had left home their feelings about him were confused. The adult world, as they saw it, consisted of 'goodies' and 'baddies'. Instinct told them their mother must be good, but if their father left their mother then crude logic told them he must be bad. But now they knew him better they could see he wasn't bad at all. Did that make *them* bad? When they hardly saw him they guessed he did not love them, but now he did. Was it in some way their fault that he had left? But he sent presents, took them to the Zoo and other places, and was always there although they could not see him. Like God? Or Father Christmas?

As the boy and girl developed, they began to rediscover their father as a man, and have an independent relationship with him. Visits to him, which undoubtedly did them good, were preceded by unmistakable tension at home with their mother. Mrs H got increasingly worried about small things, such as whether their clothes would be thought suitable by Mr H's new wife. When the children came home afterwards, they felt that somehow they ought not to say too much about the visit, because when they did their mother seemed to close up and not to want to hear. Yet at the same time she was curious about their father, and asked questions which made *them* close up. The children, as they grew older, felt uncomfortably conscious of the sacrifices their mother made for them, wished she wouldn't and felt they ought to repay her in some way. But how could they do this – other than by seeing less of their father, whose company and family they enjoyed more and more? They loved their home because they had always known it, and the years with their mother had brought them all so close that the thought of hurting her distressed them. On balance, it looks unlikely that even when these two children are sixteen and legally free to do so, they will move out and go to live with their father. But they might. And it is not difficult to imagine the effect on Mrs H if either or both of them were to do this.

Now, some years after the divorce, it does seem as if the home which these children's father could offer them might in many ways be a happier, less strained environment for them than the one which they share with their mother. No one has suggested that the custody order should be changed; but what, if anything, can be done to ease the situation? No one could say that either of these children was seriously disturbed. On the whole they do well at school and this is plainly not a case where a Children's Officer, Welfare Worker or Child Psychiatrist would be likely to be called in. Yet there are problems in this story, typical of those which to a greater or lesser extent affect the children of many divorced parents.

Let us try to look at this family more closely. To begin with, Mrs H had managed all practical matters fairly well. Two things were difficult: showing the children affection, hugging, cuddling and having fun with them, while at the same time maintaining some sort of discipline. We have said that Mrs H was undemonstrative, but the real trouble was that no one was hugging, cuddling or having fun with *her*. She had, as it were, nothing to reflect back to the children. She was lonely. As soon as she met Mr J, who gave her presents and flowers, took her out, appreciated and made love to her, she was happy. Responding to him she felt like a woman again, and it had the effect of making her behave more like a mother to the children, instead of like a composite mother-father figure who did not quite succeed in being either. She found discipline easier with Mr J in the background. She knew what she wanted of the children, and was cheerful and patient about getting it, instead of just pointlessly nagging away about nothing in particular almost all the time.

Mrs H's son liked Mr J because he mended the trains, laughed and joked so much and because he helped them to buy presents for Mrs H's birthday. He thought his mother should marry Mr J and said so to each of them, separately and seriously. The daughter was more reserved. When the affair came to an end, the boy missed Mr J's companionship and had bouts of being rude, sulky and defiant. The girl, however, was more forthcoming than for some time and plainly relieved that she was not going to be taken over by any man who was not her father. Mrs H herself felt even more lonely and unhappy than after the divorce.

Luckily the two children had each other and because there were two of them neither had to be the sole target for their mother's feelings. From comments we have heard concerning 'only' children as well as from only children themselves, we feel that the only child in a divorce is particularly vulnerable. Take William, an only son, left at the age of two in the care of his mother. His father took no interest in him at all until he was about thirteen, doing well at school, good-looking and, from the father's point of view, a delightful and admiring companion. Suddenly the father wanted to see William as often as possible, took him to watch motor-racing and taught him to use an air-gun. William naturally loved all this, but his mother, who had not remarried, found it all very hard to accept without bitterness. She had had a struggle financially when the boy was little, and had made tremendous sacrifices in order to give him a good start. She had even refused a man who wanted to marry her, because she thought William's security might be threatened by a new marriage. But she just could not compete with the range of opportunities and holidays that her ex-husband was now able to offer. When William constantly sang the praises of his newly-discovered father, she felt she was being cast off as good for nothing and no longer necessary.

In a sense, perhaps, she *was* being cast off. Parents are. Happily married people as well as divorced parents will say that at times their children seem to shut them out. Divorce, in circumstances such as we have described, merely aggravates difficulties which are probably going to occur anyway. If you cannot bear the prospect of your child growing up and becoming independent of you, perhaps you can begin to think of finding yourself some job or voluntary work. Can you fill the gap by finding other children who want loving and looking after? Or work with young people in clubs or organizations? This particular mother was really over-engrossed in her one son. As he grew older she began to rely on him for the companionship she lacked by not having a husband. To have William enticed away felt like a repetition of her husband's leaving her. Suppose any other man had offered William the same amount of attention: would his mother then have been pleased – or jealous? No mother can be a male influence in her son's life, and boys need men as well as women. They may need their father more than anyone, regardless of what he has done or failed to do in the past. School friends are very quick to spot a 'mother's boy' – and what mother really wants to admit she has produced one?

In the long term, it may help solve the problem if rather more access can be arranged. So often one hears from divorced mothers about the gifts and treats that come from the absent father, on the few, brief occasions when he and the children meet. They agonize and infuriate her, and do not always give proportionate pleasure to the children. What mothers sometimes fail to appreciate is that the expensive present is one of the few ways in which an absent father, with little access allowed, can demonstrate his love for the children. Occasionally these presents may be given in a deliberate effort to win the children away from their mother. Often they cover guilt feelings in the giver. But most often, we believe, they are a desperate, genuine, rather sad demonstration of love. If you are willing to agree to more access, perhaps there would be fewer presents. And this might help the children a lot. They and the absent parent could start to value each other for themselves rather than for anything else. Parents cannot always see this. To begin with, in the early days of separation or divorce, when feelings are raw and the atmosphere is charged with anger and bitterness, the uppermost feeling may be, 'Well, if she loved them she shouldn't have left them,' or, 'If he wants to make up for leaving them, let him give a better maintenance allowance. Then maybe I'll let him see them more often.' This is very understandable. But if over the years a mother or father can come to accept the absent parent's love for the children in the way it is offered, the children will be more likely to grow up successfully.

An important point to bear in mind when fixing access is that as children grow up their lives tend to become increasingly busy – socially with their own friends as well as at school with clubs, societies, games and added responsibility. Frequent access by the absent parent, days out, weekends away, may put a child of divorced parents at a disadvantage in leaving him too little time for all he has to do. Worse still, he may be in the position of having to make invidious choices. How can he decide between spending a day with his father or playing in the school football match? Perhaps he has the chance to act in a play, but has to refuse because rehearsals coincide with the days his father is free to see him. Or perhaps it is a swimming party with friends that has to go, or a weekend he wanted to spend at home 'just mucking about'. One twelve-year-old boy described the sheer inconvenience of having parents living apart as the thing he found most trying. 'It's all right staying with Dad, but the trouble is I don't have any of my things there. You can't take everything.'

Access, even at best, is unsettling. A child may appear to be coping with the emotional strain, but there are still the practical problems of too little time and of opportunities having to be missed. This is one of the hard facts about divorce. Parents can help by accepting it and showing restraint in the demands they make.

Children who see a spirit of disunity between their divorced parents will play on it. Of course. They are intensely practical, and if advantage is there to be taken, they most often take it. Playing off one parent against the other can happen over money: 'Mummy says she can't afford to take us to London. Can you?' Over discipline: 'We're always allowed to stay up and watch television at Daddy's. Why are you sending us to bed so early?' Over feelings: 'You don't understand me. I shall go and live with Daddy.' This kind of thing can torment a lonely, insecure parent. The more a child sees this, the more he will realize his power. Put like that it all sounds very brutal, but these things happen – with children of all ages. Where parents live near enough, a threat can even be put into practice. We heard of a teenage daughter who stormed out of the house after a row with her mother and appeared on her father's doorstep with a tale of injustice, begging to be taken in. What was he to do? Either lone parent is in a weak position in some ways as regards the children. These positions can be strengthened for both if there is real cooperation, forbearance and some trust on both sides. But it is not easy. Sometimes it is not even possible. For how is communication to be managed where there can be no trust and where parents cannot bear to meet, correspond or speak on the telephone?

When communication is impossible, either or both parents can ask the Court to authorize the Court Welfare Officer to act between them on behalf of the children. The broad outlines about how much access is to be allowed to the absent parent will be fixed by the Court. It could be half a day per week, a fortnight in the summer and a week at Christmas. Within these limits, all details about which day, what time and where the children are to be met, can be settled between the parents by the Welfare Officer, who acts as a go-between. Solicitors sometimes perform this function. To have a 'buffer' may be a tremendous help in some circumstances or for a limited time. It can also be helpful when a family of children is divided between parents who live in different parts of the country, as sometimes happens. Communication was achieved, for instance, by one separated mother in East Anglia whose husband in the West country had charge of one child, while she had three living with her. The Welfare Officer in the East contacted a Health Visitor in the West, who visited the father's house, reported on the child, and enabled the Welfare Officer to give a reassuring account to the child's mother. In that particular case it relieved anxiety, but this kind of involved communication is obviously fraught with small inconveniences. Sometimes there is need for speed – in illness or accident for example. Then mistakes can occur and letters fail to arrive. Having third or fourth parties to every decision involves time and trouble for everyone. And, of course, children as they grow up do find this kind of behaviour between adults rather childish!

Some parents find difficulty in answering a child's questions about each other or about the divorce. How, for instance, do you explain to a five- or six-year-old the prolonged absence of one of you, the fact that he or she is only a visitor nowadays? How can you explain what has happened and prepare the child for the shock of finding one of you married to someone else? Much will depend on whether your children know other families where the same kind of thing has happened, or whether this is something quite unfamiliar to them. Children easily feel rejected by a parent whom they do not see – unless the reason for the absence is something they can be proud of. When this happens, it is perhaps instinctive for a mother or father, hurt too by being left, to huddle closer to the children, in a spirit of 'We're all in this together'. It is comforting in loneliness to make an ally of whoever is at hand. But in making an ally of your child in this particular situation, respect the fact that he has feelings for the other parent as well as for you. Knowing how acutely painful rejection feels, do you really want to add to his own feelings by telling him about yours?

Most children ask their parents questions about the separation and some parents react by giving long, complicated explanations. One child may quickly lose interest, another will tell bits and pieces of the story to the other parent, who tries to even things up by giving their version. The hideous result is that the child is virtually brainwashed by both parents and becomes a kind of weapon between them. Rather than going into doubtful detail, or telling the child that the other parent 'left us because she didn't love us', can you perhaps say that the two of you could not agree about things, or get on together and be happy, and so it was better that you should part? And do not force a long explanation on a child who has asked a brief question. If he sees you really listened to the question, he will probably be quite satisfied with a brief answer, provided it is confidently given.

Avoiding unnecessary detail is quite different from putting off telling the children about the divorce because you cannot find the right words, leaving them to speculate about the odd or alarming things that are happening at home. What a child imagines from reading half a letter, seeing you in tears at the telephone, or hearing the situation talked about at school ('Jackson says Daddy is going to marry Mrs West. Will she be our mother then?') may be wildly inaccurate and fill him with terrifying doubts about the future. If he feels that you are reliable and always come home at the time you promise, if he can ask questions without seeing you embarrassed or upset by them, he can set his mind at rest. If, on the other hand, the subject of the other parent or the future, or the gossip, make you 'cloud over' as one child said of his mother, then he will not like to ask, and will stay worried and uncertain. Preoccupied with all this, he may be inattentive at school; and if the school authorities mention it you may well say that you do not think he is anxious because he does not ask you any questions. Such misunderstandings often happen.

Unhappy children who are old enough to take some responsibility are often helped by acquiring a pet, and if it makes the child an easier person to live with, it is surely worth the feeding and cleaning that sometimes devolves on you. Apart from the responsibility, pride of ownership, sheer affection for a live creature can do wonders for a rather disturbed child who is naturally fond of animals. A primary school teacher who used to take her dog to school with her remarked that although most of the children liked him, it was the emotionally disturbed ones who wanted to play with him most. You may feel a pet is out of the question. But consider carefully. You would not, after all, have to exercise a goldfish, and they are very cheap. Pets, as well as being a pleasure, are one of the many kinds of interest and hobby that help children to make new friends.

As a lone parent you will find that adult friends especially can help your children. The lone mother of sons will be wise to arrange that her children see as much as possible of uncles, godfathers, cousins and her own men friends. All these, besides the children's father, if he visits, contribute to the male image which all children need to construct for themselves, and which suffers some distortion when children live with a mother alone. Equally, a lone father whose children lack a resident mother figure can probably help them by including in their circle of friends as many complete families and as many kind, gentle, feminine women as possible. Having a variety of friends of all ages will also help to lessen tensions which arise between the generations in a small and restricted family circle.

Trouble sometimes arises early in a divorce if relatives and friends take sides in front of the children, or blacken the character of the parent who has left. It is probably done with the mistaken intention of 'showing them we're on your side, darling', but it is bound to be distressing to the child, who knows himself to be on *both* sides, and does not like to be reminded of it in this way. Friends and relatives can chiefly help children of divorced parents simply by liking and spending time with them, not by the attitudes they take up towards their parents' behaviour. Children invariably respond to older people who listen to them, show real interest and give encouragement with what they are doing. Grandparents – perhaps retired and with time to spare – can give valuable support here and will probably enjoy doing it. If, in addition, the grandparents are happily married, they can in a subtle way put back some stability into a child's idea of marriage, when his own parents have divorced.

Aunts and uncles can do the same. Cousins can play an important part in each other's lives. Not strangers or friends, not quite sisters or brothers, cousins are often the people from whom one learns what it is like to be in an age-group just above or below one's own. The boy with a friendly cousin a few years older than himself has a pattern of how to behave when he reaches that age.

Sometimes the divorce of a child's parents disrupts all sorts of other relationships which the child could have enjoyed if the marriage had lasted. This may happen for many reasons – homes too far away, too little effort made to keep up. But it is sometimes contrived deliberately. Parents keep children away from grandparents, aunts and uncles because they are afraid the children will be drawn into a full-scale family feud, 'pumped' for information, or fed with prejudice – all stemming from feelings generated by the marriage break-up. These feelings are difficult to overcome, and you may believe you are doing the right thing in severing all connection between your children and their relations. But are you sure? You will not, after all, have much say in your children's friendships as they get older. How many parents of twenty-year-olds for instance view with dismay the prospective son- or daughter-in-law who is brought along for inspection, and know full well that 'nothing we say will make any difference'?

In limiting your children in the relationships they develop, you are limiting their experience and understanding for ever. Personality grows, understanding and judgement broaden very largely from contact with other people. You may feel that your ex-husband's sister has nothing to offer, so why bring her into your child's life? But you could be wrong. You may see nothing worth while about her but your child is different. The two of them may have something in common that you do not happen to share. At least admit the possibility and let a relationship develop if it will. As we have said, children do not like being drawn into a tug-of-war which demands that they side with one against the other. They will not like the suggestion any more from relatives than they will from parents. So you probably have less to fear from 'mischief-making' friends and relatives than you imagine, and your children have more to gain from them than you suppose.

At the same time as wanting to cut children off from certain friends and relatives, a parent who is thinking of remarrying may want very much to encourage relationships with others. In the divorce situation a common difficulty is to expect too much too soon in the way of acceptance from the children. To a child of nine or ten who has thought of her mother and father as two people who are permanently there together, the idea of 'Daddy's girl-friend' or 'Mummy's boy-friend', if not positively repugnant, will take some getting used to. Your friend, anxious for acceptance and perhaps inexperienced with children, may unwittingly make things more difficult. The stranger – of either sex – who arrives with a present but does not want to see the white mice, won't play cricket and talks all through television, will not be missed if he or she never comes to visit again. That he or she might come to live seems an appalling possibility.

Be ready to help a prospective step-parent who wants to be a success with your children but who may not know how. Explain that it will take time and patience. Some people have been put off marriage by the prospect of taking on children who already have two parents. For others, re-marriage with all its new responsibilities has worked out happily. There are difficulties for step-parents. Acceptance by the children is by no means automatic, and this needs to be recognized. For one thing, a step-parent constitutes something of a threat to a child who feels possessive about a parent, and most do. The daughter who has always been the special pet of her father is bound to have mixed feelings about the new young wife who is brought into the household. In some ways, your possessive behaviour towards the children can rebound on you, for if you have restricted their friendships they can hardly be blamed for wanting to restrict yours. Even if you are not by nature possessive, divorce and loneliness may conspire to make you so. But consider: the child reported to be more disturbed than any other in her school was one whose deserted mother had first pressed close to her as her one source of comfort, and later shown that she found the child a clinging little nuisance when a new boy-friend arrived on the scene.

For a child whose home is full of anxiety or who feels torn in two by his parents, school can sometimes offer a kind of neutral ground. Here he is himself, neither 'her' child nor 'his' child particularly. Perhaps there is argument about which parent goes to the sports or who will attend the concert. In all the wrangling, what matters most is that *someone* is watching, applauding, listening to his talk, meeting his friends and sharing the day with him as well as sharing the part he plays in it. It matters very much also that you know what goes on at school. Varying with the locality and the type of school, we heard of various ways in which children of divorced parents were teased or discriminated against on account of their home background. At one level it was the primary school child's pathetic terror because 'I'll tell my Dad!' yelled wildly at the bully in the playground was known to be just an idle threat. We heard of a little girl who went to elaborate lengths to hide from others at school that her father had left home for good. She produced presents and birthday cards said to have been given by him, because she could not bear the truth to be known. And we heard of a much older girl, a teenager, who quoted a scientific fact that her father had told her, and got the retort from a classmate, 'Oh, your father wouldn't know. He's divorced.' Children vary in how they themselves treat the situation. Side by side with the passionate wish to conform, which most children show sooner or later comes the importance they feel in being slightly unusual. Thus the same child who wails 'Why can't ours be an ordinary family!' may be secretly rather pleased by the interest his family set-up causes in a school-friend – rather gratified by the eager curiosity with which he is asked 'Do your parents *hate* each other?' Explanations about who is who 'Well no she's not my mother she's my father's wife' may cause some girls embarrassment. Another says 'I keep them guessing at school about who's who!'

School authorities, headmasters and headmistresses who come across so many family situations and have such wide experience of children, are often among the wisest and kindest people to talk to about children's problems. Occasionally one finds a head of school who believes that home and family matters should be kept completely separate from the school, but fortunately in these days this is rare, and in the educational system as it is today, there will always be another authority whom you can consult. Some people feel that boarding-school, by providing a settled environment away from either parent, has much to offer children of divorce. It may sometimes be a solution to the difficulties of a single parent who is trying to bring up children as well as doing a responsible job; or for the parent who has remarried and whose children are finding it difficult to accept the replacement father or mother. Where a child shows signs of psychological disturbance, removal to boarding-school has sometimes brought marked improvement. Sometimes it does exactly the opposite. So whether it is wise for a child to go away to school depends very much on the child, and of course on the school itself.

We know, of course, that only a very few parents can afford the fees of boarding schools, but in some circumstances Local Education Authorities give financial help with boarding fees. We should stress, however, that having divorced parents, or living with only one parent who has to go out to work, is not of itself considered sufficient reason for a L.E.A. to pay a child's boarding fees. All L.E.A.s vary in their policy and in the amount of money they have at their disposal. Generally speaking, the parents most likely to receive help are those in the services, abroad, in jobs which involve frequent moving from place to place, or so physically handicapped that they cannot look after a child at home. As education authorities point out, the child in a home where married parents are in perpetual conflict may well be suffering more and be in greater need of boarding education than the child living alone with one parent after a divorce. L.E.As will not help with boarding fees for children under the age of eleven.

There are both advantages and disadvantages to boarding education quite apart from whether parents are divorced or not. Where there are frequent changes of home it can obviously be a great advantage. As a child (now grown-up) put it, 'Boarding school was the one constant factor in my life. I lived with my mother after my parents divorced and we were in a different place every holidays. She remarried and that too ended in divorce. I can't think what would have happened if I hadn't known that school would stay the same.'

To the single parent who finds discipline a problem, or to the single mother whose sons lack male company, boarding school can be a help. On the other hand, where both parents want to see as much as possible of the children, boarding school, with holidays shared and school functions divided, means that each parent misses out on a great deal as the children grow up.

Some parents coping alone for the first time find discipline a formidable problem. The sudden realization that one is without another adult to back one up in questions of how children should behave, comes as something of a shock. It is likely that the wily five- or six-year-old will want to find out just how ill he needs to look before his father – now in sole charge – decides he need not go to school. And a hefty, strong-willed girl of eleven (or almost any other age) will sooner or later want to test out a lone mother, to see what she can get away with. It is partly curiosity. Under this new, one-parent arrangement, children want to know where the boundaries of behaviour are, and how firmly they are planted. They *want* you to indicate guide-lines. To do so involves you in decision-making over difficult questions which in a two-parent home often tax the combined resources of both parents. How much freedom are the teenage children to have? Can you face the fact that they are sexual people too? At the same time, in your newly ex-married state, you may be deciding how much freedom you are going to allow yourself. How permissive is *your* sex-life going to be, and how are you going to feel about your teenager's sex-life? If what you say as a single parent seems to carry less weight because you say it alone, what you *do* will be observed far more closely by your children, simply because you and they are thrown more closely together than in a two-parent household.

Having made the decisions you have to try to stick to them, and to do so with sufficient conviction and energy to carry the day, even when you are tired or preoccupied and it would be easier not to insist. If the children see a good deal of the other parent and your two sets of ideas differ, you will also have to reckon with this. It is quite easy to become pigheaded and, because you disagree over some things, to disagree automatically over everything and feel that the other parent is bound to be wrong. Try to be objective. Occasionally you may decide to give way, not out of weakness but after careful thought.

It is very easy, when so much emphasis is laid on the harm divorce does to children, to attribute all or any of a child's problems throughout youth and adolescence, his failures and his shortcomings, to the fact of his parents' divorce. If you happen to be one of the parents you may find it easier still to blame yourself (or your ex-spouse) and feel that the child has never really had a chance. Sooner or later someone will probably say this and it will hurt you terribly. The truth is that *all* children experience failures and difficulties as they grow up, and go through phases that are agony to themselves and their elders. Divorce may accentuate these, and may in some ways make a parent's job harder, but every child, irrespective of its parents' marital state, has a potential as a human being, besides a capacity to love freely and be loved in return. These are the things that need to be cherished, and that are sometimes tragically obscured in the turmoil of divorce. Not always. In the end it is the parents' attitude, the way they feel and act, not only about the divorce itself but about other men and women, about living and loving, getting and spending, eating, sleeping and working, that will help or hinder the children in the life they are going to build.

CHAPTER 9

The 'Ex' and In-Laws

KNOWING divorce to be the end of marriage, you may think of it perhaps as a kind of artificial death– the end of a relationship which would otherwise end only with life itself. It seldom turns out this way. In general, people who have been married find it hard to bring the relationship to an end, even when they divorce. They have property which has to be divided; money which the law says they must share. They may have children who are the flesh and blood of both of them. Finally, they have feelings about each other which are liable to erupt obstinately, violently and with no logic at all. This is especially true soon after the divorce, although feelings do change as time goes by.

What divorce quite certainly does is to cut down the area of the relationship. Formerly married people vary in how much they see of one another. Some never meet. Some visit each other frequently. However this may be, the fact that they live apart makes their relationship less intimate and perpetual than it was. A couple who have slept, eaten and lived together, will only meet occasionally after the divorce, for instance at a railway station to hand over the children from one to the other. Where they once shared views about everything from their choice of friends to the number of blankets on the bed, they now share only the decision about what time to meet and at which station. They *might* share a pot of coffee if the train is late, in which case they will also share half an hour of conversation. What about? These two people know each other very well. Habits and mannerisms (she never would fill the cup to the top and she still hasn't learned to), fleeting looks that pass across their faces, make the whole experience startlingly familiar for both. What interest or importance for either of them has a discussion about the weather? On the other hand, what else can two formerly married people discuss during a chance half-hour at a railway station?

In fact they can do a whole host of things – friendly or hostile. To be indifferent, to pass half an hour together without touching each other's feelings at all, is very likely what both the ex-husband and ex-wife would most like to achieve. But few people can do this. Most of them find it harder to be indifferent to one another after divorce than either will care to admit.

No blueprint exists to show a divorced couple how they should behave with one another. Up to the day the divorce is granted there has been the legal procedure, with regulations to which they must conform. Beyond that there is complete freedom, which individuals can use how they will. The basic practical concerns which most ex-husbands and wives have in common are money and children, and these are likely to remain over the years. Money may come and go, children may live, grow up, or move away, but these things still affect both partners. How much they see of each other tends to vary. It may be twice a week or more. It may be twice a year, or less.

Feelings are variable too. They can include – simultaneously – love, hate, anger, remorse, pity – every emotion in the whole human range. So the problem confronting a formerly married couple is how to create harmony out of what they have. How do you achieve a well-balanced new relationship out of the few remains of an ill-balanced old one? How can you prevent clouds of passionate wounded feelings from the past attaching themselves to the very few things you still share – money and children? How can you stop them flowing out in the limited time you have together – half an hour in a station buffet? It happens so easily. He cannot help noticing her new clothes, and wonders if she is better off than she made out in her plea for maintenance. (Damn her, why can't she be honest?) She sees the youngest child's lip tremble as they wait for the train that will take them to their separate homes, and can hardly control her fury at the father who makes her son cry. What he doesn't know is that she borrows her sister's new coat so as to appear more confident meeting him; and what she cannot see are the tears he brushes away as he goes out through the barrier.

On the whole, people seem to find that it takes longer than they would expect for any steady relationship to develop with their former husband or wife. To begin with, both partners in their hurt pride and bitterness may behave thoroughly badly by any standards. No longer living together, they can still discharge hatred at one another in poisonous letters. They can reveal to friends, relatives, or to anyone who will listen, meanness or vice about each other that no one would have believed possible. They can – and do – recall trivial, long-forgotten incidents way back in the marriage, and point to them as the thin ends of wedges that are now plain for all to see. Not quite everyone does these things when they divorce, but many do. Very often when the crisis has passed they look back on these expressions of their personal trauma with amazement and shame. 'I can't think how I came to do such terrible things. I was beside myself with fury ...' 'I wish I hadn't talked about him the way I did. At the time I couldn't help it but I've been sorry since.'

Some people rationalize their feelings instead of just letting them burst out. Sometimes this works, but there are dangers. They may achieve what is often called a 'civilized' way of behaving, and to all appearances be quite friendly, but if their hatred or anger has not really been purged at all it will reappear somewhere, very possibly as a kind of cruelty. There is the wife who always contrives to see just enough of her husband to show him yet again that she despises him. There is the husband who gives his wife freedom, but arranges that she shall always be uncomfortably short of money. Both want to punish the other for what they have done, but find it hard to admit this, even to themselves. So each will find good theoretical reasons for punishing the other, and will use these reasons when explaining themselves to their friends. She may say 'I find I have to see him now and again – it's the only way to arrange things without long letters. And of course it saves lawyers' fees. We're grown up enough to settle this like a couple of adults.' His story will be 'If I'm to have the cash to pay for a good holiday for the children next summer we have to sit down sensibly together and work out some kind of budget.' Such stories are not necessarily dishonest, The speaker may even have convinced himself that he is telling the story the way it really is. But the anger and the wish to punish often lie somewhere beneath the words themselves.

You may look at the question of the relationship with your 'Ex' another way: why have one at all? Is not the whole point of divorce to get *away* from the other partner? Some people can get away from each other fairly easily. Mr and Mrs K married when both were students. They had no children and divorced after four passionate stormy years. The break-up of their marriage hurt both of them desperately at the time but being young they were resilient and the past they had shared was after all only a small part of a lifetime. Mr K remarried as soon as the decree was made absolute. In time Mrs K remarried as well. Mr K had no maintenance to pay as his wife was earning a good salary so they had no reason to meet and their relationship and their bitter memories withered gradually away. He saw her by chance a couple of years after they divorced, standing at a bus-stop. He was already remarried but seeing her made his heart beat furiously and wondering about her made him leave his briefcase in the bus when he got off. One evening twelve years later she recognized him in a theatre foyer. She came up and greeted him. By then all he noticed was what a lot of weight she had put on and apart from that he thought little more about her. Parting for these two was comparatively easy. Their separate lives were full and busy and after time had passed there was nothing to bind them together.

People who are middle-aged when they divorce, whose children are grown-up, and who can negotiate their financial affairs through solicitors, are also in a position of not having to meet. In this respect they may be thought fortunate; but divorce can be a very bitter experience for the middle-aged man or woman whose marriage breaks up just when old age has begun to be a frightening reality ahead. The sense of disillusionment, the blow to self-esteem, is often greater for those who have lost some of the adaptability that goes with youth. In a marriage of, say, twenty years' duration, habits have been established in every area of life. It is a mammoth task to alter these habits, to accept changes, and come to any sort of new terms with one's ex-partner. One woman, who had been married twenty-six years, said, 'My husband just left home without any warning. I've never seen him since and I never want to. I know I'm bitter. I'll always feel bitter. I can't help it.' This woman had no absolute need to see her former husband. Their children were all grown-up and married; there were no financial complications. She simply admitted her feelings and lived with them as best she could. She knew she could not come to terms with him, and did not try to do so.

A man of forty-eight whose wife left him after twenty years was so shattered by the experience that he was recommended to undergo psychiatric treatment. It was partly this treatment that helped him accept the break-up of his marriage and work through his feelings of anger and bitterness. He told us his story and we quote it in his own words:

'The relationship with my wife is a very pleasant one now. We don't live together. I see a fair amount of her. I see the children two or three times a week. I've a key to the house, but I always ask first before I come, to let her know. There's no reason why I shouldn't go there at any time, but out of courtesy I do this. The reason for the break-up of my marriage was that we were always at different angles of an emotional relationship. My wife was lively, gay and vivacious, but not very fussy about financial things. She was aggressive too. I was the opposite. I was very careful, very caring, very responsible, not very gay, not very colourful. So the situation arose that we always reproached one another for the qualities which we had looked for in the other person, but didn't possess ourselves. I complained that my wife was hopeless with money. She complained that I didn't want to do this, that and the other. These things were quite true. On that basis, the relationship had to end. Now it has ended. She felt trapped. Now she isn't trapped any more. She is separate. She leads her own life. I've established a new, very much easier relationship with my wife. There's no tension, there's no unpleasantness, and I care for my children.'

When asked if the children, aged seven and eleven, accepted their parents as united when they did not live together, he said:

'When they see us together we are united.'

'But isn't the situation an unnatural one?'

'No. It is quite natural.'

This happens to be a relationship which meets the needs of this particular couple. Both appear to have wanted it. To work it out has taken time, effort and insight that could not have been achieved without skilled professional assistance, and we do not show it as a model necessarily to be copied. Other people, quite different from these two, would probably find it an impossible way to live. But it is one couple's solution to the post-divorce problem of how to come to terms with one's Ex, when there are children whom both parents want to share.

How near to one another a divorced couple live is a factor which affects the relationship with the Ex. If you are living in adjacent streets, or even in the same town, you are fairly certain to bump into each other from time to time whether you arrange it or not. Feelings you may have when you come face to face with your Ex in the supermarket or the High Street will probably lessen as the experience gets more familiar. This could have been one of your considerations when you decided where you were going to live when you separated. Either you felt that to live close together would create an impossible situation, or you decided anyhow to try it and see if it would work. In any case the altered situation is bound to feel odd at first.

If this is your pattern and the two of you are still meeting either because you live near each other, or about the children, you will probably find that you settle into a kind of routine after a certain amount of trial and error. Progress may be slow and painful. You may meet and have rows, or be rude to each other. You may meet and end up in bed together, coming away hurt and angry, knocked right back by the encounter, the passion, and all the memories it stirs up. But gradually things will begin to settle down. Of course, if you are sickening for flu or have just ended a love affair with someone else, you will be in a low humour and are bound to find an encounter with your Ex more trying than usual. The same applies to him or her. You are still deeply involved with each other in one way because, as we have said, feelings take time to become detached. Yet in another sense, you are too little involved; neither of you knows enough about the day-to-day events of the other's life to be able to realize what is going on, or to make allowances. So it is very easy to give or take offence, whether you intend to or not.

Some meetings with your Ex may be intolerable. If you are being positively molested, either personally or by letter, you do not have to put up with this, and should seek help from your solicitor or from the police. This rarely happens, however, and it is more common to find that meetings between you and your ex-spouse are so distressing that they actually make you ill. If this occurs it will certainly be helpful to talk the matter over with your doctor, or with a Psychiatric Social Worker or marriage counsellor. The idea here is not to make you and your Ex the best of friends again. You may not want this, anyway. The point of seeking professional help is that you have feelings that you cannot control because you do not understand them; the function of the professional is to help you to do this.

One very common reason for this intense distress has to do with the reason why the marriage first started; the choice of a partner is by no means an accidental thing, but is often our way of filling a gap inside ourselves. This is why our partner is sometimes referred to as our 'other half'. We instinctively look for something that we have not got within ourselves, and find it, or think we find it, in the other person. When this dream turns out to be an illusion, the disappointment and the distress can be shattering for both partners. The whole world seems to shake, because the basis on which you have built your life turns out to be different, or non-existent. Small wonder that you are dismayed, and that your let-down is not only mental, but physical as well. Do seek help in this situation, for it is the only way towards recovery. If your life up till now has been lived on a basis that turns out to be inadequate, the sooner you are able to collect yourself and to begin again, the better for you and for your family.

Disappointment at the collapse of the relationship, instead of making you ill, may drive you to anger. No one really believes that when a marriage breaks up one side is totally in the right and the other completely wrong. Yet deep down the two people concerned *do* blame each other for what has gone wrong. They do this in spite of making generous statements about having been partly to blame themselves. What is this blame about? Is it the reflection of the disappointment we feel at making a wrong decision, at being deceived? The man whose story we have just quoted said that he and his wife reproached each other for the qualities they had looked for but did not find. Does it really make sense to blame someone else for not being what we thought they were? Is it their fault, or do we find it too hard to accept that an honest mistake was made?

This kind of resentment is very different from that of the woman in the sickening, scalding fury she feels when she discovers her husband's adultery. Then it is his betrayal, his lies and half-lies, the treachery of the other woman that she cannot forgive. That is what destroyed her trust. That is what she remembers when they meet. She vents her rage out loud, or bottles it up until it turns sour within her, poisoning her relationships with other people. A man can feel just as hurt, angry and rejected if his wife is unfaithful to him. Forgotten and buried under an avalanche of events and emotions lie the reasons which first drew these two people together – the needs that each of them hoped the other would supply.

Knowing certain things about oneself can make it an easier matter to work out a new design for living. Closely bound up with questions like, 'Why do I spend so much time thinking about my Ex?', 'Why do I always seem to fall for helpless women?', 'Why am I afraid to remarry?' are others: 'What do I lack that I hoped to find in my Ex? Do I really lack this quality?' It is for you to choose whether you leave the past alone, or with professional help try to search it for a better understanding of yourself and your present needs and feelings. It is very hard to do this alone, but professional skill has helped some people in this way, and it might help you. The psychiatrist, psychologist or marriage counsellor have carefully studied the way people feel and behave, and to them your experience is neither new nor shocking.

The better you know yourself the better you are likely to succeed in any sort of relationship with your Ex. Very occasionally former partners actually remarry each other. Surprisingly, perhaps, this is something many divorced people mention, indicating that it is also something they think about as a distinct possibility. A number of men and women told us that their former partners wanted to 'come back' or that they had considered marrying them again. We have seen some post-divorce relationships in which there appeared to be a degree of interdependence that made one feel either partner would suffer severe loss if the other should die or marry anyone else. Reactions to the death of a former spouse are often quite powerful, even when there has been little contact between them, and reactions to their re-marriage are sometimes very violent indeed. It is as though until then the way back was still open, the other partner was still available. One may know the facts; one may say, 'I think it would be a very good thing if he/she married again', and consciously mean it. But imagination and the subconscious play a great part in how one feels about one's Ex and, if you need to believe he or she is still attached to you, it will hurt you when you discover they are marrying someone else.

Relationships with the Ex are very much affected in practical ways when either partner remarries. A man may be better off financially when he no longer has to support his ex-wife, and this may ease tensions or resentments which arise over money. On the other hand, if she has children to support and she marries a man with less money than her former husband, she may ask for increased maintenance for the children, or perhaps try to get their father to pay for expensive extras for them, like bicycles or sports equipment. Neither of these reactions is likely to make for better relationships with *his* second wife, if and when he has one. So far as visiting is concerned, it is one thing for a divorced single man to go to lunch every Sunday with his former wife and their children and do all the odd jobs around the house for her afterwards, but quite another for him to go on doing it when either of them remarries. On the whole, second partners do not like their husband or wife having much to do with the first partner. The children of a former marriage are usually acceptable, but not the parent whose place the new partner has taken.

We tried to discover some of the feelings that are at work here. Is it straightforward jealousy? 'Yes,' was the reply of some. 'I don't want to share you with anyone,' was the blunt statement made by one husband to a previously married wife who wanted to go on seeing her first partner about their children. 'I don't see why I should have to spend a whole weekend boosting him up again,' said one second wife, 'after *she* has seen him and made him feel guilty about leaving her.' 'I know the power she has to get round him,' said another, 'and I don't want him talked into paying for things for her children that we cannot afford for ours.'

As one might expect, some of the most successful ex-relationships seem to be those where one person at least has a cheerful disposition that enables him or her to relate happily to a great variety of people, including a former partner. In the nature of things this type of person is likely to remarry and to be able to cope successfully with any difficulties which remarriage may bring to the ex-relationship. This does not mean that success comes easily. One woman with this disposition, now happily married to a second husband and with children of both men, sees her first husband when occasion arises – children's holidays, access visits, school functions which they attend together, and so on. She said she thought it was as hard work to have a successful divorce as to have a successful marriage. This is right, but it is worth having a successful divorce if you can manage it, rather than a bitter one.

There is a lot to be said for getting on reasonably well with your Ex, if you can. During the first months after separation or divorce, this is hard, if not impossible. And yet if you can eventually make an effort to get on together it will certainly be better for the children, and of course for you as well. The day may come when you remarry, and if this happens you will very likely want to keep on reasonable terms with your Ex.

On the whole, ex-relationships seem to work best where the former husband and wife can find a definite role for each other in the new life that each is making. If no role can be found, it may be better to let the relationship drop altogether. Where both partners are going over old ground, or where each tries to score off the other all the time, there is not much basis for happiness. The new role is likely to be limited by comparison with marriage, but if you do not expect too much of the relationship it is less likely to disappoint you.

We may sound obvious in saying that things like politeness, consideration and punctuality matter as much in dealing with one's Ex as in dealing with anyone else. It is easy to misuse familiarity, to keep an ex-husband waiting, or to let an ex-wife carry her own suitcase, just because they are ex-husband and ex-wife. If that is how you treat everyone, there is not much we can say about it, but why make an exception if with business colleagues, social acquaintances and anyone else you are punctual and courteous?

There are no rules for the way to behave with your Ex. Rather than trying to do this or that, trying to be like other people, see if you can find what is right for you and the life you are making for yourself. All kinds of details of behaviour contribute to an ex-relationship. What does an ex-wife do with her wedding-ring, for instance? From a group of divorced women, we got these answers:

'I sold mine.'

'I wear it.'

'I threw it at him.'

'I let my boy-friend throw it in the Serpentine.'

'I keep it in a box and it looks at me sometimes.'

Other major contributors to the picture of your divorce are your in-laws, the family of your Ex. Jokes about mothers-in-law are numberless, and if you have always had a variety-gag relationship with yours, it is not likely to improve with your divorce – except by ending altogether. In a marriage between people of different religious or vastly different social backgrounds, divorce sometimes brings relief to everyone concerned by making it unnecessary for people who have nothing in common to go on trying to like each other. But sometimes people develop very happy relationships with their in-laws, and divorce then inevitably causes some clash of loyalties. If a man advises his brother's ex-wife about money matters, will it be seen by the brother as a blow against him, a criticism of what he has done? Should she get help elsewhere, make a point of leaving her former husband's family alone, as though to keep up with them were poaching on his preserves? It is a matter which requires some tact and also some thought. What are your real motives in keeping up with your in-laws? Are you wanting them to judge between you and your Ex, to tell you that you are a splendid person and deeply wronged? Very likely this is what you want. You want approval – who doesn't – and approval from them will be especially valuable, because it could have been expected to belong to your Ex who is their kith and kin. Their support for you is very reassuring. In keeping up with in-laws, however, it is as well to remember that they *are* the family of your Ex, whereas their relationship with you is more of a privilege on both sides. It may be tactful to keep away from your in-laws until emotions have calmed down, or until they have shown that they want to keep up with you.

Where there is real affection it is everyone's loss if this is neglected or ignored. Where there is a real friendship it will often survive in spite of a divorce, even if for a time there is not much contact between those who share it. Many divorced women, and some men, told us of the practical help and support they had received from in-laws. The pattern in these cases was generally that the family of a partner who left to marry someone else, befriended the one left alone, or alone with children. For the children to lose not only a parent, but grandparents, aunts, uncles and cousins seems very hard and scarcely necessary. Where a mother-in-law or father-in-law really feel they have acquired a son or daughter through marriage, one that perhaps they never had of their own, to lose him or her may make a sad difference to life. It is not just a matter of filling the gap with the next person their son or daughter marries. One daughter-in-law said that she felt a responsibility towards her ex-husband's elderly mother, who was a lonely person with no daughter of her own, and had come to rely on her understanding over the years. She could not imagine walking out on the old lady, and so she continued to visit her after the divorce. If there is some point of contact with the in-laws apart from the Ex, if people share the same interests, enjoy the same things, there is always a basis for continuing friendship, provided that feelings are not too complicated or intense.

The mother and father of your Ex are not only your in-laws, they are the grandparents of your children. Even if you do not get on very well with them, the children may love seeing them, and may very much miss the relationship if you force it to an end. Sometimes a husband or wife, to pay back their former partner for what they have done, denies access to the children by their grandparents, saying:

'All right, I'll show them what they get for supporting their precious son (or daughter). If that's the way they are going to behave, my children ought to be protected from them.'

We know that it is possible for some in-laws to discuss the marriage problem with the grandchildren, but very few would really do this. By separating your children from their grandparents you can be cutting off your nose to spite your face. Your children may well need all the care and love they can get at this time, and forced separation from their grandparents may be yet another burden that they are ill-equipped to bear.

Sisters- and brothers-in-law are likely to have much less complicated feelings than parents or grandparents about a divorce in the family. For one thing, they are of a different generation; if there is prejudice it is likely to be in the older person rather than the younger, and of course change of any kind takes longer to accept and get used to as one gets older. In addition there is the fact that parents naturally have parental feelings, and these remain very strong even when children have grown up. Few parents, particularly mothers of sons or fathers of daughters, can bear to see their child hurt, or admit that he or she is in the wrong. Instinctively they want to blame someone else, to find a scapegoat. Some partly blame themselves, but the most obvious person to take the blame is the daughter-in-law or son-in-law, or in a triangular situation, the man or woman who appears to be breaking up the marriage. Parents may say, like everyone else, that there is right and wrong on both sides, but the hurt they feel for their own child will make them angry with *someone* – and it could be you.

Sometimes there is two-way anger. Mrs L's husband was a gambler. Mrs L had tried to help him get over this weakness which she felt was a result of the way his mother had mismanaged him as a child. When she realized she could not alter him, and the perpetual uncertainty about money became more than she could bear, Mrs L left her husband, whose mother made out that he would never have gambled to that extent if Mrs L had made him happy or looked after him properly. There was a history of jealousy between these two women and the divorce only aggravated it. Mr L's father, on the other hand, who was separated from his wife, always liked Mrs L and they used to meet from time to time after the divorce, and even after Mrs L's remarriage.

Remarriage tends to weaken ties with ex-in-laws rather as it weakens ties with your Ex. As life goes on and one gathers new relatives and new friends, some old ones lose touch and fall away. A second marriage may bring a second family of in-laws, and new partners are inclined to resent a husband or wife continually harking back to people and things associated with the first marriage. Once again you have a choice. You can keep in contact with your in-laws, seeing them when it suits you both. Or you can let the relationship dwindle away until the in-laws of your former marriage belong to the past.

CHAPTER 10

Sexuality and You

WHAT are you expecting of this chapter? Have you turned to it first to see what we have to say about sex? Does sex mean to you the act of sexual intercourse? Are you wondering how divorced and separated people behave sexually, and what may be expected of you? Are you checking to see whether your feelings and behaviour are normal?

Sex is not what you *do* with or to another person. It is what you *are,* a man, a woman. Your sex is not simply your occasional, frequent, or non-existent physical relationships, it is your maleness or femaleness. We will make ourselves more plain if we speak of your sexuality rather than of sex for we believe it is much more important to see and understand the whole sexuality of a person than to limit ourselves to a discussion of sexual intercourse. Not that we want to avoid the real issues and problems arising from the sexual drives and needs of mature people who no longer have a partner. We want to deal with them, but we see them as a part, not the whole, of what it is to be male or female.

Your sexuality governs the way in which you react to things, to people, to ideas. It affects the way you drive a car, the kind of films or plays that make you laugh or cry, the way you feel about babies, about young children, about teenagers, about parents. It is not in any sense something to be ashamed of. Indeed without your sexuality you would be very much less interesting than you are. What is vital to you is the way you use your sexuality, and this will depend on what you know about yourself, and on what you have learned to expect of other people. To give an example, many boys are taught from an early age that 'little boys don't cry', but that little girls are different. They have been told by other boys, by their parents, or by someone else, that boys are supposed to be tough, that although it is all right to comfort a girl by putting your arms around her, boys have to be told to 'pull themselves together'. The boy who has been told and who believes this will grow to be ashamed of his tears, to hide his need to be comforted. He may tease or torment other boys who get upset, who are seen in their mother's arms, or being kissed by their fathers. But little boys do cry, do need to be comforted: communication by touch is quite as important as by words, and the child who has been taught to avoid showing his emotions may later find that he has difficulty expressing himself as a sexual person, as a man.

To know about your sexuality, to be aware of the way you feel as a man or a woman, is to gain the means to control the way you live. Your knowledge of yourself enables you to make a choice about the way you behave at home, at work, and sexually. And it seems to us that this capacity to *choose* how you will behave is the greatest asset you have. The way you exercise choices, especially in relation to other people, is part of your personal morality. 'Morality' is a difficult word; it can be understood to imply some kind of worthiness, a 'good' quality that we all ought to possess. This is not the way we mean it. The way you act affects other people, makes them happier, more miserable, gives them joy or brings them despair, boredom or passion. Thus you are responsible for what happens to them. This is a fact, not an opinion.

How does this responsibility relate to our sexuality? And if responsibility is just a matter of fact, where does morality come into it – if at all? We think that the more you know about yourself, the more aware you are of the fact that your actions affect other people, the more you are likely to act in a way that will satisfy you and them. So we are not trying to lay down any kind of moral code. It would not help if we did. We are telling you that you do have a choice in the way you will act in relation to other people. You do not have to act in the way you think, or fear, everyone else behaves. And the way you exercise your choice will make a lot of difference to the satisfaction – and the pleasure – that you will find in your relationships.

Part of your view of yourself is founded on the way that other people react to you. It has been said that 'a woman defines a man', and it would be equally true to say that a man defines a woman. You find out who you are in your relationships, and you will tend to treat people according to the way you think they value you. This affects the quality of your relationships with the opposite sex. If a man thinks that all women see him as a pitiful creature, maybe because this is the way one woman says she saw him, he may try to punish every woman he meets. If a girl thinks that men see her only as an object to take to bed, she will get what she can from them, giving as little in return as she need do.

Mr M had passed through half-a-dozen affairs with women in as little as six months, most of them people who were working at his office in the City of London. His divorce had made him distrust any permanent relationship, and he saw these partners simply as conquests, tributes to his masculinity, to be left behind when he was ready to move on to better things. Like most men who use relationships this way, he only found temporary satisfaction, and was always looking for someone new. He soon got a reputation which fitted the way he was behaving and, although he was still able to do his job, he could find no one to talk to at the office. After a time, the other men seemed uninterested in his sexual conquests. He thought that this might have been due to their envy, and laughed at them to himself. What was more difficult for him was to get the girls at the office to flirt with him the way he liked. Eventually he found himself going around with just two of the girls, both of whom had expensive tastes, and when he was passed over for promotion at the end of the year, he began looking round for another job.

What had happened to Mr M was his gradual isolation, caused by his own unwillingness to make close relationships with other people. Sexually, most other men found him irritating, some because they would have liked to have had the same sort of sexual adventures, others because they could see nothing interesting about him as a person. The girls at the office talked about him, and word got around that he was no kind of matrimonial prospect; he would have agreed with this – marriage was the last thing he was looking for; but the result was that the 'market' became restricted, and the only girls who were willing to go with him saw him as a man who would provide entertainment and an expensive evening, in return for twenty minutes in bed at the end. This was the bargain they struck, and he soon found himself in a blind alley, having to move on to other work because he could make no progress or gain any satisfaction from his job.

Mr M's story sounds like a cautionary tale, and it is, but of course this does not mean the end for him. It might well be that this experience will make him think about the reason why he was unable to make progress. He may decide to avoid close relationships with anyone at the next job, keeping his social life separate from his work. Even this would not provide a complete solution, for he will probably still find the work sterile; a man who decides to avoid close contacts with other people rarely finds that they take much notice of him. If he is lucky, Mr M may find he meets someone whom he can trust enough to listen to him while he talks about himself, and who will help him think out what he really wants to do, and what kind of person he wants to be.

Mr M has a choice. He can shut himself off as a sexual person, giving and taking nothing. He can go on with the same pattern as before, moving quickly from girl to girl. He can start a search for the kind of relationship that will be more than sexual, for a girl who can spend the whole day with him without his feeling that sexual intercourse has to come at the end, like the full stop at the end of a sentence. Mr M, and all people who are divorced and separated, do have a free choice in the use of their sexuality. You can (and some do) enter into full sexual relationship with anyone who appeals to you. You can leave sexual intercourse alone altogether, trusting neither yourself nor other people in a physical contact that disturbs you so much. Or you can begin to use your sexuality rather as you do your intelligence, making thoughtful choices and understanding more of the way that you feel. You will soon find out, if you do not know already, that there are no rules for sexual behaviour among divorced and separated people. Some are promiscuous, some abstain altogether from sexual intercourse. Some express their sexuality in solitude, others seem to spread themselves across the whole social range.

So what guide-lines can we give you? We have said that no one has yet made any rules. If you want to have intercourse with several people, or just with one person, you may be able to arrange it. If you want to leave sex alone altogether, this too is easy. In fact, it is the very extent of the choice that is so confusing, and for some so distressing. For a woman, it may mean that she will have to alter her image of herself before she can satisfy her sexual drive. We think then, that the most effective guide-lines will be the ones that you develop for yourself. Try thinking of it this way:

What sort of a man (or woman) am I?
What kind of people do I like, and have I always liked that kind?
How do I feel about the other sex, and why?
Is the way I feel simply the result of the marriage I have just been through, or is there more to it than that?
Do I want people to like me, to respect me, to find me sexually attractive?
Do I expect them to be that way, or am I surprised when they are?
Do people trust me? Do I trust them?

You can even write down your own reactions to questions like these, and find out a bit more about yourself. This will help you to make choices about the way you behave. In the first place, you have more *time* than you think. There really is enough time to make up your own mind. If you are put under pressure to start a sexual relationship today, tomorrow, or next weekend, you don't have to react straightaway. You can say that you want to think about it.

Divorced people usually find that the sooner they sleep with someone the sooner they will be alone again. The more thoughtful and selective you are, the better the chance of a longer and more interesting relationship. It sounds almost comic to say that sexual intercourse is a unique experience, but it is true. In most situations we are in fairly close control of ourselves, but as the excitement and drama of sex play builds up this is less and less true. Most people, especially those with a good deal of satisfactory sexual experience, begin to have increasingly dramatic feelings as they begin to make love, starting perhaps in their heads but soon spreading to their sexual organs. Intercourse is much more than an orgasm, it is a growing physical contact that, when it is satisfying to the man and the woman, moves to a crescendo of abandonment and release.

Although the patterns are rather different for men and women, the mounting feelings are much the same, and the feeling of satisfaction too. The trouble is, it is so easy to fall into the trap of thinking that it is all a matter of technique. Hundreds of thousands of men and women read anxiously through books about sex, wondering whether their own technique is good enough, whether they will be thought to be 'good in bed'. In truth, one of the greatest things about sexual intercourse is its potential variety. Some men and women like to have powerful, passionate relationships, the man carrying the woman upstairs, throwing her on to the bed, stripping her clothes off and going quickly to an orgasm that is overpoweringly exciting for them both. The people next door may prefer to be much more quiet; the man may telephone during the day to ask her how she is; she knows that this means he is asking her if she would like to make love that night, and by the way she replies she will tell him, not necessarily in so many words, how she feels about the idea. When he gets home he will kiss her a little differently than he did last night; after supper they may settle down to look at the television, only touching one another lightly until, some way through the evening, they make love quietly on the sofa.

We said there were no external rules laid down for sexual behaviour, and this is just as true for the way people make love. They can, and they do, please themselves. Some couples like to behave the same way each time they make love, others prefer variation. Passion may be all right one night, gentleness the next. And of course what suits one person may revolt another. If you have a very rigid expectation of what sexual intercourse is, or should be like, then you must be prepared for some very real problems. One man liked to make love secretively, always in the dark, and almost as if he was someone else. He would even turn on the light afterwards and pick up a book or listen to the radio. This had worked fairly well with his wife until the last year of their marriage when everything, sex included, had gone wrong. After the divorce, he went to bed with one or two women who seemed to like him and who were content with the way he made love to them, but his third encounter was quite different; the girl insisted on having the light on, told him to keep his eyes open all the time, to talk to her while it was happening, and it ended in disaster for him and disappointment for her when he was not able to complete their lovemaking at all. It was almost as if they were speaking a different language, and neither could understand what the other wanted. He left her flat as soon as he could, and tried to avoid meeting her again.

There is no 'moral' to this story; the man was not 'wrong' and the girl 'right'. We are not suggesting that he should go out and start practising a new kind of sex-life. Maybe his existing way of using his sexuality is best for him, and he should stay that way. What he could learn, though, is that he cannot expect everyone to speak his sexual language straightaway, if at all. A child born in Devon will speak English, with a West country accent; another child born on the same day in a fishing village on the northern coast of France, not many miles away, will speak another language with a local accent of his own. If they meet they will have something in common, they will be able to communicate in some ways, but it will take them a long time before they can understand one another at all well. Sexual language is much the same and we should no more require people to behave the way we do than we would expect a foreigner to speak our language. The sexual language which we first learnt is the one we will use – at least until we have been taught a new one. If we are introduced to sexuality by seeing violence and passion on the films and on television, we may expect that this is the way we ought to behave in bed, and our first sexual contacts may be coarse and insensitive. If we have seen people – maybe our own mother and father – loving one another in a gentle way, this will be our own expectation of the right way to express our sexuality.

Some people are afraid of their sexuality, discovering that there are forces within them that they did not expect and cannot control. So when we feel like singing, or want to speak to total strangers, or feel passionate emotions that we have never before experienced, we are shocked and even afraid.

In fact, although fear of one's sexuality is perfectly normal, there is no need for it. Strong feelings are absolutely normal. So are feelings of tenderness. Some people go through periods of wanting to avoid all sexual contact, while others seem to be under regular pressure to express themselves this way. It is only rarely that a couple find that they are on exactly the same wavelength in the way they express their sexuality, but if they are able to talk to one another about it they will find that they can solve their problems without difficulty. Sometimes though, the whole business of explanation is too difficult.

A girl may find it quite impossible to say in words how much she likes one way of making love, but how she dislikes another. She cannot talk about it at all, because she is too embarrassed to bring up the subject and knows she cannot find the right words. A man may wonder anxiously whether he is pleasing a woman sexually; he will ask her, 'Was that all right?' – and the simple answer 'Yes' may leave him wondering whether she is just being polite. He wants to know whether he is able to evoke a response in her, and only if she can put her feelings into words will he become confident enough in himself as a lover to be able to offer her even more. This is where it is important to know that there are many ways of communicating. Words are not the only method. The way a man looks at a girl while they are out together, the way she holds his arm as they cross the street, the way he drops his voice when he wants to say something tender to her, all mean something more than can be put into words. It is just as well; if we were limited to words to express ourselves we would miss a whole range of expression, and be emotionally poverty stricken.

If you think that you do not know much about this sort of thing, think again. You know a lot about how the boss is feeling when you get into the office, just from the way he opens the door, grunts 'Good morning', or drinks his coffee. You get a clear idea of the waitress's mood at lunchtime from the way she takes your order, puts the plate on the table, reacts to the way you speak to her. You can read sexuality the same way, provided you are willing to notice what the other person is feeling, and why. Watch what they do, not furtively, but naturally and openly. Look at the expression in their eyes, the way they lean forward, the tone of their voice. These things are just as important as the words they use, and by noticing them you are increasing your range of communication with the other person, because the way they react will depend on what you see, how you feel and what you do. Communication is a two-way process, a kind of understanding between people. You will be much happier with your sexuality if you can learn to use it, to interpret the messages that other people are giving you. Learn to receive messages as well as to send them, and you will find that you can make the choices we have been talking about with much greater ease.

It is easy to see freedom of choice as if it were nothing to do with morality or with responsibility. In fact, we believe these things are inextricably linked with one another. At the beginning of the chapter we discussed responsibility, and the clear fact that our actions do, whether we like it or not, affect the way other people feel and the way they behave. The question is, what are we going to do about this (rather uncomfortable) fact? If a man takes a girl out, treats her well, gives her small presents, she will almost certainly begin to feel better about herself – and more fond of him. She may start to build castles in the air around their life together, to let herself fall in love with him. If a woman helps a man with his practical problems, washes his clothes, listens to his stories about work, lets him make love to her from time to time, he may begin to see her as the one person who can solve all his problems. Now it may be that these feelings are appropriate, that each partner *is* beginning to respond to the other in much the same way. If so, they will very possibly come closer and closer to one another until they are ready for the permanent relationship of marriage. But suppose that the man had no strong feelings about the girl, only wanting to please her, enjoying her company but intending no permanent relationship? Suppose the woman had washed his clothes because she felt sympathetic, had allowed the man to make love to her because she did not want to offend him? If this happened, then two people are due for a crushing disappointment; and it may well be the second such disappointment they have suffered in quite a short time. If so, they may feel destroyed and rejected, driven into a deep depression from which they may be unable to emerge for many months, or even years. Is this the kind of reaction we want to produce? Are we totally indifferent to the way that someone else is going to live their life from now on? There can be very few people who are so detached that they can look with complete indifference at the way their own actions have affected other men and women. Only a sick person can take any real pleasure from the destruction of another's confidence. So it seems to us that the great majority of normal people will want to consider not only what they are and how they feel, but also how their actions affect the people they are with. The way we treat the next person we meet says something about us; the way we see ourselves affects the way we act, and the way that other people see us.

CHAPTER II

Sexual Sanity

How are you going to use your sexuality? Just as you are bound to be concerned about the way to bring up the children, balance your budget, manage your home and develop your career, so you will need to think about the best way of expressing your sexuality. This can be done. Your sexuality does not operate only below your waist; it is not just a matter of your sexual activity, although that is bound to come into it. Your satisfaction will come from knowing about yourself, being aware what suits you and what does not, whether you like close relationships with a few people or friendly contacts with many, or both.

Pay no attention to those who tell you that you are expected to do this or that, must sleep with your current partner on or before the third date, must be bright and social to have a chance of meeting interesting people, must achieve sexual satisfaction early in a relationship if it is going to work out. Rules of this kind simply do not apply to everybody, and the area of choice is wide indeed. Think first of sexual intercourse with the opposite sex. The choice you have is infinitely wide. It seems to us to range between abstinence, promiscuity and selective activity, and although we cannot tell you which to select we can give you some idea of what each will involve.

If you decide to abstain from intercourse you may have many good reasons. You may still have strong feelings for your former partner, and not want to think of yourself in the arms of another person. This is not only natural, but very common among the divorced and separated. Some people, badly damaged by the collapse of their marriage, are quite unable to think about physical closeness with someone else. This is particularly true for those whose former partner has hurt them badly by saying that they are sexually inadequate. In fact, when this is said it can be the exact opposite of the truth, for the person making this kind of remark is often trying to shift their own feeling of guilt on to their partner.

There are others who prefer to abstain altogether from sex because it creates such havoc in their emotional lives, preventing them from thinking calmly about other things. People like this may have major decisions they are trying to take, or are building up a new career and want to concentrate all their energies on this one thing. All these reasons for deciding not to have intercourse with anyone after your separation or divorce, and many others, are perfectly valid. The really important thing, though, is to know why you decide this way and try not to delude yourself about it. Easier said than done? Yes, but you can work it out if you take time over it. And though the real reason for the way you behave may be tough to face, you will feel better after you have faced it. Think, for example, of the man who is afraid of impotence after being faithful to just one woman for many years, and who cannot think how to cope with someone new. He may try to convince himself that his reason for abstinence is that he does not find women attractive, or that he has lost all interest in sex. The more he tries to convince himself the more troubled he will be, but if he is able to think calmly he will see that his lack of confidence, very possibly only temporary, is reasonable and understandable. It has in fact been shared by many others like him. Also, it is perfectly possible for a man and a woman to have a close and mature relationship which does not include sexual intimacy. Knowing this will help him to live with the problem until it either solves itself or at least becomes less acute.

Some people go to the other extreme, and opt for as much sex as they can get, with anyone who is available. This is known as promiscuous behaviour. We think on the whole that promiscuity is more a symptom than a disease. Most men and women who act promiscuously seem to us to be trying to prove something about themselves, to show that they are attractive, lovable, or just good at it. We doubt that this is what they really prove. You will meet quite a lot of men like this, and some women, who claim that they find a promiscuous life highly satisfactory. They are usually the people who talk most about it, which means that in fact they are far from sure of themselves. In fact, the ability to make enduring relationships is a mark of maturity, of sexual sanity, and the 'butterfly' behaviour of promiscuity shows a good deal of uncertainty and anxiety. Therefore we cannot condemn it; we can only hope that the promiscuous will find a way out of a pattern that reassures very few people, and that some even find rather boring. If you see friends behaving promiscuously and wonder whether they are having a much better time than you are, there really is no need to worry; even if it seems to suit them it will not necessarily suit you. Being hooked on sex can be something of a handicap.

Selective sexual activity is the middle course, and from what we have learned it is the one that most divorced people follow. They do sometimes have intercourse, but not often and certainly not with everyone they date. They make a careful choice, based on the way they feel about the other person after getting to know them fairly well. They may decide to live together for a while. For very many people, physical intimacy is an expression of their warmth, affection and love.

Again, we have no guidelines to offer, for we are not concerned with what you *ought* to do, but there is no need to worry about being abnormal or wildly immoral if you, as a person who has been very used to regular expression in intercourse, need to continue this from time to time, with someone whom you respect and like, and may come to love. The morality, as we see it, lies mainly in what you are doing to the other person rather than to yourself. Think hard and long before you enter into a sexual relationship that you are taking fairly lightly, but that the other person feels about seriously and deeply. You can scarcely want to hurt or damage them, nor do we think that you are likely to be indifferent to what happens to them. So it seems to us that you will need to think more about the other person than yourself. Selective activity is not the same as occasional activity; it means giving thought to a relationship in which two people have feelings, and in which at least one can get badly hurt.

You have become used to having intercourse fairly often in marriage; you may have come to enjoy it very much, and be missing the feeling of relaxation and well-being that most people have who are sexually fulfilled. Therefore you cannot respond sexually in quite the same way as you did before you were married. In the first place, the partner you are with probably knows that you have been married, and naturally expects you to be sexually experienced. The same may be true of him – or her. When two people, both formerly married, are out with one another, each will inevitably wonder whether and when their relationship will become overtly sexual. It is the experience of most divorced people that when sexual intercourse does take place between them, there tend to be fewer preliminaries than there are with the unmarried. Anxiety centres not so much on whether or how often the other person has had sexual experience, but on the particular techniques or behaviour that they are going to expect. Knowing that intercourse is both common and expected by some divorced people need not lead you to behave the same way. You have the right to pause and to discover yourself again. You may very well decide that you want to remarry, and that until that day comes you will be content to wait.

For many people, sexual activity with someone other than their husband or wife makes them feel very guilty. This is expecially true if they made their marriage vows in church and feel that they should stick by what they then said, even if their partner has not done so. Others feel guilty, not so much on religious grounds, but on account of what other people, their parents, neighbours, friends or children may think of them. If you are going to feel this way it is much better that you should think very carefully before you enter into any kind of sexual relationship. Although feelings of guilt are not always justified, nevertheless they are absolutely real, and if you behave as if they do not exist you will probably suffer more than by leaving sex alone, at least for a time.

Suppose, though, that the idea of intercourse with someone else does not disturb you. This does not mean that you will want to have it with anyone. How do you decide about this? First, we think you should find out quite a lot about the way he or she behaves outside the bedroom before you go inside. This is bound to take some time, but it is going to be worth it. Is she really interested in you, cares what you have to say, or is she only putting on an act for your benefit? Is he prepared to let you think for yourself, does he intuitively sense some of your concerns, or is he only working out the way to get your clothes off? Difficult questions to answer, because the better the act a person puts on, the harder it will be to know him or her at all well. All the more reason why, if you have doubts, you should leave things awhile.

Some people are best avoided. If they show a pattern of moving quickly from one relationship to another, never being able to settle with anyone, if they seem only able to talk and not to listen, if they are quite unaware of the way you feel, then it will be better to stay a little distant. The chances are that they will move on to someone else quite quickly, and that you will forget one another. Also, unless your own needs are very acute, it will be best not to go to bed with someone who seems to be in a great hurry. It is easy to make a mistake sexually not only because of your physical needs but also your emotional needs. If you feel you have been rejected by your married partner, you may badly need the reassurance of close bodily contact. Yet if you act too quickly, hoping against hope that this time it will be different, there is a real danger of disappointment. One book for divorcees stated quite plainly that:

> 'One answer to the question of how attractive you are is just to go out and see.'

But we believe that this is not only wrong but cruel. First, you may be an attractive man or woman without being outstandingly magnetic sexually, and secondly, you expose yourself to the worst of disappointments if you believe that the behaviour of the first person you meet gives any real idea of your value as a man or a woman.

Another reason for giving a relationship time to develop before plunging it into the fast-flowing river of sexual activity is that it will probably affect your reputation. We know from experience that many men and women talk to one another about their sexual partners. Perhaps this applies more to men than to women, for they often have a greater need to exhibit their sexual 'successes', and get pleasure from comparing their performances with one another. A woman who goes casually from man to man, then, is likely to become known as 'available', or as an 'easy lay'. Very few women really want to be thought of this way.

We have been discussing sexual intimacy with other divorced and separated people, because this is the way it usually happens. But not always. For the man or woman who is separated or divorced while still young there is the possibility of going around with unmarried people. This does not necessarily present any particular problems, though you may find yourself with a stronger feeling of responsibility with someone who is not yet married. For him marriage is still something ahead, a permanent relationship of which he knows very little. For you, marriage may mean a bitter experience, and you may be tempted to show that this is so. Be well advised and keep these feelings to yourself. Marriage is capable of developing into the most satisfactory relationship that can exist between a man and a woman, and indeed the great majority of divorced people are still hoping that this is something they will one day be able to achieve – with the right person. For this reason, you will need to go carefully with unmarried friends, and not destroy their own hopes and dreams with cynical remarks about marriage.

Then there is sex with a married man – or woman. For obvious reasons this is going to raise difficulties, and will very likely lead to unhappiness, certainly if your partner is still living with his or her spouse. We know very well that sexual intercourse happens this way often enough. Nevertheless, the odds are against you if you start an affair with someone who is already married, especially if they have children and do not want to be parted from them. However attracted you are, think hard about the future and the likelihood, for that is what it is, that you will ultimately be left alone at the end of this kind of affair. It is a hard truth that, as you get older, the best mates are already married, and the better they are the more reluctant they will be to damage the lives of those around them, however fond they may be of you.

It is hard enough to take the decisions relating to your sexuality and the extent to which you are willing to express it physically with the opposite sex, but the problems are by no means solely personal. They are practical as well. If you want to have intercourse with someone, it will have to be arranged at a convenient place and time. This is not always easy, especially if you have children, or live in circumstances where people are likely to see you and your friends coming and going. As we have already explained in our chapters on Managing and Money, and as you may already know from experience, the practical situation of many divorced people is very difficult, and they may have many problems finding a suitable place to live. Even when you have this it may be hard to achieve any kind of privacy. For these reasons, it can be difficult to arrange for a sufficiently intimate setting in which intercourse is possible, let alone enjoyable. Landladies hover with disapproval, flat-mates return at awkward hours, neighbours call in unexpectedly. If you are looking after children you may be able to go out for part of the evening, but you will have to be back in time to relieve the baby-sitter. An American author has said:

> Putting the matter in the most awkward way possible, given the boudoir facilities, working hours, and social relationships within any given clique or circle, a couple must carry out detailed and clever plans if they wish to continue a sexual relationship without eventual marriage. The divorcee consequently finds any given arrangements short of marriage increasingly inconvenient.

A man and a woman had known one another for some time. Her teenage children seemed to get on well enough with him, though the girl was rather distant in her manner. One evening the children went out together to a party, but returned unexpectedly, asking for the key which they had left behind by mistake. Although the children did not see either their mother or her visitor undressed, the man was in the bedroom and could not very well hide the fact. The children soon left again, but their mother was so distressed and embarrassed that she was quite unable to go any further with the sex she had planned. She was mortally afraid that her daughter would form a bad opinion of her, and the one thing she did not want was for the girl to become promiscuous, which she feared might happen if she herself appeared to be behaving in the same way. The strain was too much for her and the man, who stopped seeing one another. No harm seemed to have been done to the children, as it turned out, but their mother never got over the experience and avoided close relationships with anyone else, for fear the same thing might happen again.

It is difficult trying to hide one's sexual needs from the children. They do not like to think of their parents as sexually active people; this is true for the children of most marriages, let alone those from broken homes. So what are you to do, especially about your teenage sons and daughters? It seems that the best way to act is to make it clear that whilst you do not want to shut your friends off from the children, you too have a life to live. You want to go out sometimes, you want to be able to spend a little money on yourself, to choose your own friends, to live a private life. The children want this too, and the older they grow the stronger their wish is. If they can see the similarity to their own situation they will be more willing to accept the private part of your own life.

There are not only your children to be considered, but your partner's. This situation develops more often for the man than the woman, and he can easily find himself not knowing quite what to say to her family. The older they are the more difficult it is. The most important thing to remember is that her children have a very close bond with her, and need her attention and care just as much, and probably more, than you do. They have a life with her that is going to be part of them forever, and they will almost certainly be jealous of her relations with you. This is the way things are, and you cannot change them. Do not start competition to take her attention away from the children and give it to you. Just be as sensitive as you can to the way they feel. Be prepared to move out of the way now and again, to accept that she needs and cares for them just as much as they need and love her, and you will find that she will also have time for you as well. The same is just as true for a woman who is meeting her new partner's children; they have a bond with him that she will want to recognize and respect, and she will understand that they need to take up some of the time that she might really prefer him to spend with her.

What of your feelings of jealousy, especially of your partner's former husband or wife? Many people find themselves drawing comparisons, especially sexual ones, between their own performance and that of their new partner's former mate. A man may wonder whether he is as good at arousing the woman as her husband was, especially if she talks about that aspect of her life with pleasure. A woman may find herself wondering, while she is in bed, whether the way he makes love to her is the way he used to do it with his wife. This is not necessarily a problem that can be discussed until it is resolved, although discussion may help. The former partner is a fact of existence, may still be keeping in touch for various good reasons connected with the children, and it is best to accept this, if you can, as part of the past that can no more be denied than can your own previous experiences, whatever they may be. Jealousy of this kind can be all-consuming, and it is best to look it square in the face, accepting the facts as they are or have been, rather than mulling them over and spending hours in anxiety and recrimination.

Sexual sanity is not easy to develop. Our deepest emotions are involved in our sexuality, our evaluation of ourselves, our hopes and our fears, memories and expectations. We grow up with a host of impressions about sex, starting from the day when we first learn that men and women do something to, or with, one another before a baby is born. If we are lucky, we learn about this at home in a natural way, but just as likely we will make our first discoveries about sex and reproduction from young friends whose knowledge is at best inaccurate and often really misleading. We have been surprised to discover how many divorced people know little about the sexual facts of life and about contraception. You really owe it to yourself to know how you are made physically, how you and the opposite sex function sexually. Find a good but reasonably short book or booklet (see page 195) and you will be surprised at the number of misunderstandings you have, even now, about the sexual facts of life. Learn, too, about contraception. People who have intercourse without taking contraceptive precautions are not merely taking risks with one another; they may create a new human being in circumstances where it would have been much wiser to have made sure that no child could result. The man who expects a woman to deal with the contraceptive precautions as a matter of course is not merely naïve – he is thoughtless. If a man wants to have intercourse with you and gives no thought to the dangers of conception, ask yourself whether he really cares for you very much.

For those whose religious belief allows the use of contraceptives, there is a fairly wide choice: medical opinion seems to be agreed that the contraceptive pill, taken by the woman, is very effective, as is the sheath, or condom, used by the man. Other methods range from foams and rubber caps inserted in the woman's vagina to plastic and metal devices, and the ancient method of 'withdrawal', which is well known as the least effective of all. Normally it is best to take medical advice before deciding on the best contraceptive method, and you can get this from your doctor or from the nearest Family Planning Clinic.

There are on the market a mass of books and booklets, some illustrated and others not, dealing with all aspects of human sexuality. Some sell at very high prices, and are produced for the pornographic market. Others are for the medical prefession, and there is a wide variety sold between these two extremes. There are books dealing with masturbation, sexual techniques, positions in intercourse, male and female homosexuality, perversions, venereal diseases and so on. We will take a little time to discuss these, mainly to put them into perspective. First, take masturbation, one of the most common of sexual activities. It is very unusual for a young man or woman to have had no experience of masturbation, which occurs when you bring yourself to a sexual climax instead of waiting for someone else to do so. Responsible medical opinion is agreed that masturbation does no physical harm, as was once alleged; it is a normal outlet for the sexual instinct, and like many activities it only creates problems when it is indulged in to an excessive degree. What is exessive? This varies from person to person, and even when a man or woman is masturbating daily it does not do them any serious harm. It can, however, have some effect on one's interest in responding to the opposite sex, and in men it can also introduce a feeling of lassitude which is rather inconvenient. There is absolutely no need whatever to feel guilty about masturbating; it is a normal habit, less enjoyable than sexual intercourse, but harmless. It cannot be recommended without reservation, but there is no need for the massive anxiety and guilt that has surrounded it over the past hundred years and more.

Really serious are the venereal diseases, the most common of which are gonorrhoea and syphilis. In serious cases, especially when not treated, they can result in permanent damage, sterility and even death. They are caught by having intercourse with someone else who is suffering from the disease, although risks are slightly reduced by the use of the male sheath as a contraceptive. If you have intercourse with a new partner, then you are taking a risk, albeit a small one, that you may contract venereal disease. The less you know about him or her, the greater the risk. It is as simple as that. If you have any pain, any discharge, from your sexual parts within a few days of intercourse, then it is absolutely essential for your own protection and that of other people to obtain medical advice and treatment. You should also name your sexual contacts (which you can do in complete confidence) to the V.D. Clinic you attend, so that the disease will not be passed on from person to person.

One very common way in which venereal disease is caught is through male homosexual activity. The chances are that you will not have had very much if any contact with homosexuals, but if you have done so you will know that they prefer sexual contact with members of the same sex. For the promiscuous homosexual, and many of them are this way, there is a continuing risk of contracting venereal disease. For the normal heterosexual person, the homosexual can be rather disturbing, not only because his habits seem unnatural, but because some male homosexuals behave in a very overt and effeminate way. Homosexuality is not a disease or a sickness; it is a condition which varies in its intensity and its symptoms.

There are also female homosexuals, commonly called lesbians. Divorced women say that they do meet lesbians from time to time, but as with male homosexuals, they create no particular difficulty and are not likely to give you any trouble. If you find that you have some homosexual interests yourself of a mild or less mild nature, there is no need to sink into despair or anxiety. If your feelings cause you difficulty you should seek medical advice. If you are interested in reading more about the subject, there are inexpensive paperbacks that will help you to become better informed.

There are a few people who act in a way that society regards as sexually perverted. Perversion is very hard to define, because different groups regard differing actions as being perverted. For instance, there are some who consider that oral-genital contact (during which the mouth of one person touches the sexual parts of the other) is a perverted action, and also intercourse in any position other than the one in which the man lies on top of the woman. Others think of these and other forms of heterosexual contact as not only normal but thoroughly enjoyable. We think it is more or less impossible to draw the line one side or another of what is perverted and what is not. What we would say is that, if a particular action suits you and your partner and you both enjoy it, then it is really not the business of anyone else what you decide to do. This applies only, of course, to those who are adult and responsible for their actions; it is generally agreed that the sexual exploitation of the young is antisocial and must be prevented by law.

There are many publications on the market describing sexual techniques, positions for intercourse, sensitive areas of the body, and so on. In themselves they do little harm, and some people may find them interesting and helpful. Sadly, though, the numbers of them that sell, and the way in which they are advertised, indicate that they are produced more for sexual titillation than for information. Details of sexual techniques used in tribal societies, in cultures on the other side of the world, of initiation ceremonies and of bizarre sexual behaviour, all go towards making us think of our sexuality as peculiar, dirty or shameful. Small wonder, then, if we find it hard to be calm about sexual behaviour or feelings.

A man left his wife five years after they married. She was sexually experienced before they met, and when the marriage began to go wrong she began to pour scorn on his sexual performance, telling him that he was hopeless in bed. If this was true, it was she who had made it so. He drifted for a year after the separation, too frightened to approach another woman sexually, for fear of similar scorn or rejection. Then he met a cheerful plump girl who was not really his sort at all, and who had almost nothing in common with him. He had a professional qualification, and she had never passed an exam in her life. He took her out several times, just because she made him feel cheerful, and one night after several drinks they went to bed together. She was generous and friendly, and while she was not in any sense in love with him she helped him to put away his feelings of sexual inadequacy. When their relationship came to a natural end after a few months he had thrown off the effects of his poor marriage and was able to re-establish himself and his masculinity. He was, and still is, very grateful to her.

We have discussed homosexuality, venereal disease and perversions because there is a chance that you may come across them at some time. But do not let the fringe problems of sexuality lead you to become afraid of your own masculinity or femininity. There is nothing intrinsically wrong about sex, just as there is nothing wrong about your appetite for food. It is what you do with your sexuality and the way you use or respect other people that will govern your satisfaction and your feeling of identity.

CHAPTER 12

The Future

ONLY when the present has finished throwing problems at you can you begin to think about the future. You may have found somewhere to live, have fought or compromised the legal issues, discovered ways of making ends meet. The children may be settling into their new way of life, becoming used to access days or visits to an absent parent. You may be coming to terms with your own sexuality, discovering more about yourself and starting to put your divorce behind you. Now what? What about the next five, ten, or twenty years? There is no urgent need to make decisions today that will affect the way you live from now on, but you may want to start thinking about the future, and about the sort of life you want to lead. There will be choices, if not now then in a few years' time. You can begin to plan for a different kind of life, but this will be hard for you unless you know the general direction in which you want to go, and also the extent of your independence.

We think that independence is a state of mind rather than a state of fact. It is something which comes to you gradually as a result of having to make your own choices and act on your own decisions. You may find that being on your own allows you more time to read, reflect and listen, so that the views you hold about all sorts of things – politics and religion as well as sex and morality – mature, deepen and even alter. This does not mean that you always have to think and act in isolation. We exist in relationships with other people, and one of your choices comes in deciding how much to lean on other people and when to branch out on your own.

Another choice you undoubtedly have is whether or not you want to remarry. Remarriage is society's short answer to divorce – the still possible happy ending for the man or woman whose first marriage breaks up. Public opinion on the whole disapproves of divorce, dislikes its image and tends to react strongly against the husband or wife who leaves a family to go off and marry someone else. Once the idea is a reality, however, and the gossip has died down, society will accept more readily the person who remarries than the one who remains alone. This is a fact and we have already discussed some of the reasons for it. To men and women divorcing without immediate plans for remarriage, it poses the problem of finding a place for themselves as individuals in a society that likes couples. If social pressure is on the divorced to remarry, how do the divorced respond? Some marry again as soon as the decree is made absolute. Others remarry as a result of being divorced but within a comparatively short time – say one to three years. Some take much longer and some never remarry at all.

Age has a good deal to do with remarriage rates, the peak age for remarriage being thirty to thirty-four for men and twenty-five to twenty-nine for women. The situation confronting a man who wants to remarry after divorce is rather different from that which confronts a woman. Men, in our society, are at present in great demand; they are scarcer than women and they tend to have a shorter life-span. If a man wants a wife, with every year that passes his choice widens, since he can marry a woman any number of years younger than himself. His income is probably increasing steadily until retirement, and his ability to have children does not normally cease even after that. The divorced woman's position is almost the exact opposite. As she gets older, though she may not lose her attractiveness, she will have to stand competition from younger women as well as from the many in her own age-group. At the same time her choice of husband gets more limited because women do not normally marry men much younger than themselves. In her case, income probably will not alter with age, so this is not likely to have much effect on her chances of remarriage. Moreover, the children from her previous marriage and a decreasing number of child-bearing years ahead may easily count against her.

On balance, men do appear to have a greater freedom when it comes to remarriage. On the other hand, if they are already supporting a former wife and/or children, the choice may be rather narrower than at first appears, for financial reasons. Mr P, for instance, aged forty and with an ex-wife of thirty-eight and three children to support, fell in love with Mrs R, aged thirty-four, divorced, unsupported by a foreign husband and with three children from her first marriage. She made it clear to him that if she married him she would want children – she was that kind of woman. The prospect of seven children to support, with at least four of them actually living in the house, made him reluctantly decide that he simply could not marry Mrs R. The decision when it came surprised them both, because neither had ever thought that for them something as mundane as money could really affect anything as romantic as love.

Both of them had preserved many of the feelings they took into their first marriages and were ready to apply them to a second. But they had reckoned without their responsibilities and without certain facts about their own feelings which had become clear as they got older. To her, marriage to a man she loved meant having his children, and over this she knew she could not compromise. He knew himself sufficiently well to realize that he could not – even for a woman whom he loved – put up with a lot of children on the low standard of living which was all his income would allow.

This aspect of second marriage – that it is often a decision made quite as much with the head as with the heart – surprises a lot of people and even shocks a few. Where some people feel that even a second-best relationship is better than living alone, others, embarking on second marriage, sometimes feel there must be something wrong this time because there is not the glamour or excitement or recklessness that went with their first marriage. Where one partner has already been married and the other has not, there has to be mutual understanding over many things – for a start how each feels about the actual business of getting married. A man or woman not long divorced may want to cut down on the formalities of getting married a second time, whereas the new bride or bridegroom may want to enjoy them to the full. Although there can be no white wedding in church where one partner is divorced, there can still be a reception and a honeymoon. But now these may depend on how much money is going out in maintenance to the first wife, or whether anyone can be found to look after the children while their mother is honeymooning. Anxiety and nervousness, a last-minute feeling that you cannot go through with it, are very common among people remarrying. The intensity of these feelings may be quite incomprehensible to someone marrying for the first time.

'If you're so worried about marrying me, it must mean you don't have confidence in me, and that makes me lose confidence in myself,' said one man to a recently divorced woman whom he wanted to marry. His loss of self-confidence led to violent jealousy of the girl's first husband, which showed in the way he treated her children (their father's name was not allowed to be mentioned) and in his possessive attitude towards her. The situation became impossible for everyone and they did not marry. Possibly, with more time, more patience and a better understanding of post-divorce feelings, the deadlock might have been avoided.

Despite these and other difficulties, each year thousands of divorced men and women do marry people who have not previously been married at all. Many second marriages are very happy; mistakes made in a first marriage are not always repeated, and people often attribute the success of their second marriage largely to experience gained in the first. In some ways the divorced may be more down to earth than the single about the practical aspects of marriage; they may be more determined to keep a second marriage together and consequently work harder at it. Where there are children there is responsibility; but responsibility, though it may discourage recklessness, need not kill romance. We know that for some people, romance that was sadly lacking in a first marriage, comes resplendently with a second. Mrs S, for instance, an only daughter, married when she was very young, soon after the death of her father. She married a man considerably older than herself, whom she admired and genuinely believed she loved. Five years later, Mrs S met and fell passionately in love with another man who just as passionately wanted to marry her. He was about her own age, unmarried and prepared to take on the children. Her husband seemed suddenly too old, too dictatorial and she began positively to dislike him. Mrs S's second marriage, after divorce, was a tremendous success, and she felt the first had happened only because she was so young and in a specially vulnerable state at the time.

This girl was made vulnerable by the death of her father, but divorce too makes people vulnerable. There is a very real danger that those who have a great need to remarry will rush with no clear thought into what looks like a romantic second marriage, only to find later that it is a ghastly mistake. In the deluge of happiness that comes to them when they fall in love, they not only forget all they know of themselves and their responsibilities, but may also form a very biased impression of the man with whom they are in love. It is a picture made up of the qualities they most *need* to find, and because their need is so great they attribute these qualities to the person they have actually found. To some women, badly hurt by desertion, another man's tenderness and love are so healing and reassuring that they will close their eyes to everything else about him. If, as well as being attentive, he is also on the way out of what he describes as a bad marriage ('My wife just doesn't understand me'), the new woman may feel drawn even more strongly towards him. Family and friends who shared her unhappiness at the time of the divorce now see a marvellous change brought about by the new man. They conclude that he must be 'right' for her and so encourage a marriage which is quite possibly not the best thing that could happen either for her or for the man.

Most people like to think of marriage as essentially romantic even the second time around, and the suggestion that it can have any other basis strikes them as disappointing, disgusting or just plain dull. Whatever one's feeling, the fact is that spontaneous romance is *not* the only basis for marriage. There are others. And if you have gone through divorce and are wanting to marry again, it is surely worth taking a look at some of them.

To the incurably romantic, the thought of going to a marriage bureau, where for a fee one can be introduced to a number of suitable partners, may seem unpleasantly coldblooded. Another feeling is that there is something shameful about trying to find a husband or wife in this way. Yet often the very people who say this will privately assess everyone they come across as a possible marriage partner; they will look eagerly round any gathering – chance, business or social – in fairly obvious search of a mate, or join a Divorced and Separated Club with the sole aim of finding one. To the systematic or single-minded person who is keen to remarry, marriage bureaux are an obvious possibility. They now exist in a number of towns in this country as well as London, where the first started operating just thirty years ago. Some people even consult a bureau when they are still thinking about separation, to find out what are their chances of remarriage should they decide to divorce. Some others, after divorce, go to a bureau regretting that they cannot find a partner for themselves but feeling that if the thing is on a commercial basis, at least success must be guaranteed. It is not. Anyone who decides to sign up with a bureau – however reputable – should do so in the knowledge that though they *may* be helped to meet a possible husband or wife, they cannot insure against disappointment.

Mrs T was twenty-eight when she and her husband divorced, and after three years in which she continued to look after her children, and established herself in a job, she began to feel that she was missing a great deal by living alone, and started wondering how best to set about finding a second husband. She had a good many married friends and came across a few people in connection with her work, but she hardly ever seemed to meet marriageable men of a suitable age. A friend who had met her own husband through a well-known bureau suggested that Mrs T should try the same one. Partly out of curiosity and partly for fun, she agreed to do so. On application she was sent a friendly letter asking her to come to the bureau's office for personal interview, having first filled in the fairly long form enclosed with the letter. This asked for particulars about her age, appearance, income, occupation and interests as well as details about her first marriage, how many children she had, how much time they spend with her and so on. Another section asked what sort of man she would like to meet, single, widowed or divorced, whether she would want children and if she would consent to live abroad. There was a section which included a number of more general questions, such as what was her attitude to smoking, drinking and entertaining and whether she would enjoy taking up new interests to share with a partner. Finally she was asked to describe her own personality.

Mrs T had thought quite a lot about remarriage, but always vaguely. Supplying positive answers to specific questions helped her to realize some of the issues that would be involved. She realized too that until now she had been thinking of the future in a very negative sort of way. All that had gone wrong in her first marriage was so fresh in her mind that in picturing a second, she had thought a lot about what she wanted to avoid, and not much about what she hoped to achieve. The interview at the bureau when it came was informal and friendly, and Mrs T decided that it would be worth registering in spite of the £10 fee which was the charge at this particular bureau. Immediately after her divorce she could not have afforded this sum, but now it was just possible and she had begun to see the whole thing as an important step in planning her own future. There were others; she joined two clubs where she could pursue her favourite hobbies – photography and painting – as well as a swimming club where she could take the children.

Mrs T did not marry any of the several men she met via the bureau. Some time later she married a man she met in a different way altogether. But she still reckoned that the bureau had given her valuable experience and that her money had been well spent. She had had introductions to a number of men whom she would otherwise never have come across. Furthermore she had met them on equal terms, not because she was someone's wife, or someone's mother or the woman who did a certain job at the office. Gradually she was able to meet strangers without nervousness, and to be more interested in getting to know them than in putting over an impression of herself. When, initially, she had described the sort of man she wanted to meet, Mrs T had had enough common sense to realize that such a man was not likely to be on the bureau's books and quite possibly did not exist at all. None the less, she had stated and thought about the qualities she would really value in a new partner. If you do this you will unconsciously watch to see how people match up to your standards, and judge for yourself accordingly. If, for instance, you know you want a partner who is honest, if you have made a positive statement about this, then you are likely to notice signs of dishonesty in any man or woman you go out with. If, on the other hand, you are hungry for love or sex and have never thought much about honesty, you will probably let pass the odd lie as you relish the fun of a day or the close intimacy of a night. After that it will be much harder for you to disentangle facts from the feelings which by then may have started to run away with you and to cloud your judgement.

The chief thing Mrs T came to realize through her experience with the marriage bureau was that her need to remarry was less than she had believed it to be. She could have married some of the men she met, but the fact was that though she liked them and enjoyed their company she did not want to marry any of them. Immediately after her husband left her, and for some time after her divorce, she really thought she would marry any body rather than nobody. This is one of the extreme reactions to divorce. The other extreme, of course, is the feeling that you never want to remarry under any circumstances at all. Although most people experience one or both of the extremes to begin with, in time they usually adjust to somewhere between the two. We asked the director of one marriage bureau if she agreed with us that a period of 'quarantine' following a divorce might be a good idea before embarking on a new marriage. She said she thought it would be excellent, and suggested about two years as being the shortest time it took most people to settle down emotionally, and to be ready to start a creative new marriage as opposed to a hastily staged repetition of the last one.

The proportion of first and second marriages which break up is much the same. This may sound encouraging to the man or woman who is hoping their second marriage will endure; but statistics can be no absolute guarantee for individual cases, and it is worth mentioning that we met a solicitor who told us she had women clients who had gone through a second divorce having made the mistake of marrying someone very like their first husband.

An obvious pitfall in making a second – or third – marriage is that of marrying someone with the same qualities which combined with one's own have brought disaster in the past. There is the type of competent, efficient, hard-working woman who is always attracted to the ill-disciplined, untidy, unsuccessful man, whom she longs to organize and reform. She may succeed, but there is a strong possibility that he will come to hate her for it, and that she may begin to feel a martyr to the task she has taken on. Yet if the marriage breaks up she may well go and find another similar man and start the whole process again. Then there is the kind of man who is attracted by a much younger woman; she grows up during the marriage and ceases to be what he wants so he goes on looking for younger and younger women. There is the man or woman who falls in love with one person after another – usually with the same physical appearance – and each time hopes this will be the real thing. Some people like this avoid marriage altogether and keep their relationships on a more fleeting basis. They sometimes feel they have the best of both worlds: close companionship and the possibility of falling in love again. It is rather like making time stand still so that it is always Christmas Eve and never Christmas. Some people, though they know the type of person they would be wise to avoid, do not know what to look for instead. They cannot embark on a new marriage, and in their loneliness drift in and out of emotional situations with one person after another.

A future of loneliness stretching away for ever is the private nightmare of very many divorced people – particularly when the situation is new. They may find it hard to believe that as time passes and problems are overcome, much of their loneliness will be transformed by their increasing independence – their freedom to choose confidently, and that this is something even they may come to regard as precious. What does independence mean to you? Does it mean being able to support yourself financially, or not having to consider anyone else? Perhaps it means being free, able to choose where you live and what you do. Perhaps you think of an independent person as someone who knows all the answers and never gets cheated or hurt. Perhaps you think of him as eccentric, a rebel, a law unto himself. Independence may mean all of these things or it may mean none of them. We think that you are independent when you feel independent, and not until then.

In our society we are taught from an early age that financial independence is a desirable thing. You may understand this to mean being able to support yourself, or being free from worries about money – not bound by financial considerations. No self-respecting man or woman enjoys being financially dependent, partly because it is looked on in our society as an admission of weakness. On these counts divorced women strive for financial independence from their former husbands. What the husband wants is something rather different. Still the chief breadwinner, even after divorce he wants sufficient money to enable him to keep his former wife and/or another without inconvenience.

There is also what we will call social independence, and we see this as the ability to meet other people as and when it suits one's individual needs. Shyness, lack of confidence or just lack of effort can all contribute to throw divorced men and women in on themselves to a point where a life that is largely fantasy seems more satisfactory than the non-life which reality seems to offer. We all have dreams and fantasies – some of us more than others. When life is unbearable, those who can withdraw from it may be counted lucky; their dreams keep them going. But dreams, like opium, are addictive and the person who first withdraws for protection may find himself before long living almost entirely in imagination – dependent on his fantasies. He talks of doing things but never does them; he thinks he has certain feelings but they are never put to the test. Other people find they know less and less about him because he shows nothing of what he is really like.

Everyone depends to some extent on other people's understanding and therefore on meeting them and communicating with them. Custom and habit sometimes restrict the social life of someone newly divorced. You are used to a certain type of social life and for some time it is very hard to accept that you may have to seek the society of other people in new ways. If one is going to remain at all balanced, the company of other people is essential. If in the past a woman has relied on social events connected with her husband's job as her chief means of meeting people, after divorce she will find herself bereft not only of drinks and dinners but also of human company. The result is that divorced women often feel they are social outcasts, and conclude – mistakenly – that since they have no husband, to be an outcast is inevitable. They are not social outcasts; with time, they may be able to get to know quite a lot of people and to build up a busy social life, but it will come about in a different way. One woman who had been divorced some time told us that she advises any newly divorced friends to accept every opportunity for meeting people that comes their way. She had done this herself, and said that although sometimes the opportunities offered looked pretty meagre and unexciting, and she found herself going to functions she would never have bothered about when she was married, things often turned out unexpectedly, and she developed a capacity for enjoying everything in some way or other.

'I entertain far more than I am entertained,' another divorcee told us. A third put it this way: 'If I give a party, then I get asked back by other people. But if I don't make the effort I should never be asked anywhere.' Her explanation was that many married couples and families with children are busy and self-sufficient and do little in the way of entertaining. Those who do, often hold a conventional attitude about inviting people only in pairs – like animals going into the Ark. To them a single woman is a complication because a single man has to be found to make things even, and this is not always possible.

Giving a party costs money. Even having friends to supper costs something and on a really tight budget this is either impossible or unmanageable on the scale the hostess thinks would be appropriate. In former days the same friends were entertained better and she feels that the hospitality they offer in return will be embarrassingly good. To this we can only say, try it and see. You will soon discover the people with whom you can share a friendship despite the differences in your economic positions. There is no point at all in trying to keep up with the Joneses or anyone else unless you really like them. If you do really like them, keeping up in that sense will not be necessary. Part of the meaning of friendship is surely that you *care* for your friends and they for you. There will be times when they will want to do things for you, and other times when you can do things for them – not necessarily the same things. A couple living in a seaside town who lent their house to a divorced girl so that she could have a holiday, had their kindness repaid some years later when the same girl gave a room in her house to their son, who by that time was a student and had nowhere to live.

Women on their own sometimes complain that they are at a greater social disadvantage than men on their own. A single man, they say, is always counted a social asset, but single women are two a penny. We talked to one divorced man with an extremely busy social life who gave another side of the picture. 'It is very depressing,' he said, 'to be continually asked out when you know perfectly well that it is because you are a social asset and not because you are a valued friend.'

Sorting out your friends, establishing your social independence, can be a rather painful process if you end by finding you have not got many friends whom you really like. You can always make new ones if you are prepared to reach out to people, care about them and enjoy them. In fact, as an individual without the restrictions that marriage inevitably brings, you have immense opportunity for a very wide range of friendships indeed. And the chances are that the friendships you make in your independent state, with people of both sexes, will be deep and lasting.

There is no doubt that many people who divorce make a thoroughly good job of being alone because they feel independent. Necessity drives domestically helpless men to manage a house and bring up children; it drives women to become graduates, best-selling authors, business promoters and do a host of other things they never knew they could. The successful, independent individual is often envied for this very independence. Society tends to see these people as secure, able, well-organized, worldly-wise and toughened by experience to the point where they cannot be hurt.

Many people who start by being desperately lonely do experience a great sense of happiness and achievement as they reach a state of growing independence, realize their freedom and use the opportunities it offers. But if these are the rewards of independence they are also its dangers. We see loneliness and independence as opposite points on a compass; as you travel away from loneliness you go towards independence, but if you go on travelling you will reach loneliness again. Some people say they do not want to remarry and lose the independence they have found since being on their own. Sometimes this is said with a hint of regret, and one wonders if the person saying it feels that in achieving such freedom they have lost some of their power to adapt, to change and to share. Freedom, however desirable, is not an end in itself. By all means learn not to depend on your children for affection, but do not in the process become so insensitive that you no longer value their affection when you have it. Certainly develop the capacity to manage money, the home, a social life, but do not become so isolated that you cannot accept any kind of help. The over-independent person, who is rigid, self-sufficient and uncaring – however successful in the eyes of the world – can be as lonely as the deserted husband or wife in the first stages of misery and rejection. So also can the people who find most difficulty in reaching a state of independence, but manage instead to put on a rather aggressive show of self-confidence.

Between your first loneliness and your final independence many factors will go to make you a more experienced and in some ways a different person. You may have lost the future you once thought was assured; but you have learned that there is another future – one that you can create for yourself.

Useful Books and Booklets

Many of the subjects we have discussed here are dealt with in more detail in other books. There is a list of these below, in each case with a brief note about the contents of the book. Most of them are reasonably priced in paperback editions. If you have any difficulty buying them, your local library will probably be able to get you a copy of the book or books in hardback.

Children

CASTLE, *A Parents' Guide to Education*, Pelican Original, 25p. (Written for parents to introduce them to teachers, school governors and administrators.)

ELLISON, *The Deprived Child and Adoption*, Pan, 17½p. (A full account of the services available for children in difficulty, and their parents. Practical notes about adoption.)

INGLEBY, *Students away from home*, National Marriage Guidance Council, 25p. (Useful book for anxious lone parents of teenage children.)

MILLER, *Careers for Girls*, Penguin, 80p.

RATCLIFFE AND REED, *Parents under Stress*, National Marriage Guidance Council, 25p. (Simple booklet for parents worried about handicapped children.)

SPOCK, *Problems of Parents*, Pan Piper, 25p. (Written sympathetically from the parents' point of view.)

Careers

JOHNSON, *Working at Home*, Penguin. (To be published Autumn 1972.)

LABOVITCH AND SIMON, *Late Start – Careers for Wives*, Cornmarket Press, 40p. (The best book on this subject. Optimistic – and helpful.)

Food and Drink

BRIGGS, *Entertaining Single-handed*, Penguin Handbook, 25p. (For people trying to work out the practical side of making a new social life for themselves.)

H.M.S.O., *ABC of Cookery*, 25p. (For people who have never had to cook for themselves, and who may now be trying to live on tinned and frozen foods.)

Housing

NATIONAL CITIZENS' ADVICE BUREAUX, *Buying a House or Flat*, 12½p. (Deals with the more simple legal and technical aspects. Useful for those who have previously lived in rented accommodation, or with in-laws.)

VICKERS, *Buying a House*, Penguin Handbook, 25p. (Discusses all aspects of house buying. Full of excellent advice.)

Law

ANTHONY AND BERRYMAN, *Legal Guide to Domestic Proceedings*, Butterworths, £1·50. (Expensive but good guide to matrimonial and other action in Domestic Courts.)

Money

NATIONAL SAVINGS COMMITTEE, *Value for Money* (Money management book No. SL 370. Available free from local office of National Savings Committee.)

CONSUMERS' ASSOCIATION, *Money 'Which?'*, Quarterly magazine available on subscription from 'which', 14 Buckingham Street, London, WC2. (Up-to-date ideas about money.)

CUMMINGS, *Investment*, Penguin, 25p. (Advice on all ways of investing your money.)

DAILY MAIL, *Income Tax Guide*, 17p. (Excellent summary of highly complex tax legislation. Published annually.)

GILLING-SMITH, *The Complete Guide to Pensions and Superannuation*, Pelican Original, 52½p. (Very full and comprehensive, though fairly complicated to take in.)

H.M.S.O., *A Guide to Social Security*, 35p. (Detailed and comprehensive.)

Personal

DOMINIAN, *Marital Breakdown,* Pelican, 20p. (A very good summary by a psychiatrist of the main causes of broken marriages.)

NATIONAL MARRIAGE GUIDANCE COUNCIL, *Parents Growing Old,* 25p. (Practical help for those having to care for older relations.)

SMITH, *Woman in the Middle Years,* British Medical Association, 10p. (Straightforward and factual. Deals with the menopause.)

WILLANS, *Inside Information on Conflict in Marriage,* Dickens Press, 25p. (A study of current stresses in marriage, and much advice on personal problems.)

REED, *The Woman on the Verge of Divorce,* Nelson, £1·80. (By the Publications Officer of the National Marriage Guidance Council.)

Professional and other Services

WILLMOTT, *Consumer's Guide to the British Social Services,* Pelican, 40p. (Admirable guide, giving very much more detail than covered in Chapter 5 of this book. Very well indexed and absolutely realistic. It tells you what there is available, not just what there ought to be.)

Sex

BEVAN, *Sex – the Plain Facts,* Faber, 30p. (This book is just what it says it is. Short and clear.)

BLOOM, *Modern contraception,* Delisle, 20p. (Up-to-date summary of all the methods available.)

HARRIS, *Questions about sex,* Hutchinson, 30p. (Covers much the same ground as Dr Bevan's book, but lighter in tone, with rather less technical illustrations.)

HEGELER, *The XYZ of Love,* Mayflower, 50p.

NATIONAL MARRIAGE GUIDANCE COUNCIL, *Sex in Marriage; Sex in the Middle Years; Help with Sex Problems in Marriage,* 25p. each. (Don't think that the Marriage Guidance Council booklets are only for married people. These three make just as much sense to the formerly married, and they keep off moral overtones. The third booklet is especially useful to those who have sexual difficulties but don't want to talk about them.)

Sex Education

HEGELER, *Peter and Caroline*, Tavistock, 35p. (The best book for young children, eight and under. Well illustrated, and absolutely clear.)

POMEROY, *Boys and Sex*; *Girls and Sex*, Pelican, 20p. each. (Frank honest, clear, and completely up to date. Strongly recommended for the young teenager.)

Some Useful Addresses

Advisory Centre for Education (ACE), 32 Trumpington Street, Cambridge, CB2 1QY. *Tel.* 0223–51456.

Family Planning Association, 27 Mortimer Street, London, W.1. *Tel.* 01–636 9135.

Legal Aid Department, The Law Society, 29 Red Lion Street, London, W.C.1. *Tel.* 01–405 6991.

National Citizens' Advice Bureaux, 26 Bedford Square, London, W.C.1. *Tel.* 01–636 4066.

National Federation of Clubs for the Divorced and Separated (N.F.C.D.S.), 13 High Street, Little Shelford, Cambridge.

National Federation of Housing Societies, 86 Strand, London, W.C.2R OEG. *Tel.* 01–836 2741.

National Marriage Guidance Council, Rugby, Warwickshire. *Tel.* Rugby 73241.

The Salvation Army, 101 Queen Victoria Street, London, E.C.4. *Tel.* 01–236 7020.

Samaritans, Pinewood Road, Iver Heath, Bucks. *Tel.* Iver Heath 4421.

Index

MORE ABOUT PENGUINS AND PELICANS

Penguinews, which appears every month, contains details of all the new books issued by Penguins as they are published. From time to time it is supplemented by *Penguins in Print*, which is a complete list of all available books published by Penguins. (There are well over three thousand of these.)

A specimen copy of *Penguinews* will be sent to you free on request, and you can become a subscriber for the price of the postage. For a year's issues (including the complete lists) please send 30p if you live in the United Kingdom, or 60p if you live elsewhere. Just write to Dept EP, Penguin Books Ltd, Harmondsworth, Middlesex, enclosing a cheque or postal order, and your name will be added to the mailing list.

Note: *Penguinews* and *Penguins in Print* are not available in the U.S.A. or Canada

A PARENTS' GUIDE TO EDUCATION

E. B. Castle

Does a child's home environment determine his intelligence score? What sort of people are teachers? Is there a real parents' choice? What is a school for?

These are just some of the questions which parents face, and which are answered in this clear and readable guide to education by the author of *Ancient Education and Today*. Always conscious of the ideals in schooling, this is yet a realist's book and illustrated by personal experience. E. B. Castle begins by tracing the most formative ideas in the British tradition of education, and describes how they have influenced teaching methods and teachers' attitudes towards children. He goes on to discuss social problems such as equal educational opportunity and the effect of environment on intelligence. Later chapters deal with the future of schools, what type of people the staff should be, and the internal organization of a school.

Written primarily for parents, to introduce them to teachers, school governors, and administrators, this book also introduces teachers to themselves and young teachers to their profession.

Also available

ANCIENT EDUCATION AND TODAY

WORKING AT HOME

Joanna Johnson

With housework to do and husbands and children to look after, thousands of women need a wider outlook on the world, and extra money also, and may often have wondered how best to occupy themselves during the little spare time they can find. Joanna Johnson describes many of the things they could do and how best to do them. Here are some of her ideas:

Kennels and boarding
Rabbit keeping
Mink
Assembly for factories
Child minding
Baby-sitting
Freelance cooking
Making jewellery
Making soft toys
Embroidery
Gardening
Mushroom growing
Bee keeping
Wig making
Home help
Insurance collecting
Journalism
Washing and ironing
BBC audience research
Proof reading
Sub editing
Beautician
Dressmaking
Knitting
Teachers' aides
Translating
Literary typing
Commercial typing
Helping the disabled
Helping the elderly

Joanna Johnson (housewife and 'home worker extraordinary') sets out to answer the questions 'What can I do? How do I start? What are my chances of success?'

BUYING A HOUSE

L. E. Vickers

A concise and comprehensive account of how to buy a house (or flat).

Where to look for a house.
How much will it cost?
How to deal with estate agents.
How to deal with solicitors.
Where will the money come from?

The author gives as examples two main income brackets (one couple can afford a house in the region of £4,500, the other £7,000 or more) and takes us through every step. All the details required are here – the financial and the legal, the building societies, the estate agents, solicitors and surveyors. Methodically Mrs Vickers outlines the various ways of raising money and the intricacies of conveyance and explains the force (or weakness) of a deposit, the meaning of 'freehold' and 'leasehold' and the rights of sitting tenants. On a less legal level she urges caution about the winter aspect of houses viewed in summer and other pitfalls, and reminds purchasers of all the terminal arrangements to be made for moving day.

Those embarking on the exciting process of acquiring a new home could have no better guide: for the author, as well as having a sense of humour, has a flourishing practice as a solicitor.

MARITAL BREAKDOWN

J. Dominian

A marriage collapses. Psychology, sociology, and medicine may say one thing: religion and law pronounce another. In this study, probably for the first time, a psychiatrist has made an unbiased attempt to bring together these different viewpoints. How do men and women select their partners, asks Dr Dominian. And what are the factors that break a marriage up – sex, money, housing, parents and families, mental illness, or the inability to give and take emotionally? Do such influences as age or pre-marital pregnancy count?

The author makes no inspired guesses in answering these questions and is chary of ready-made solutions. Proceeding from the latest research he simply indicates the places where a deeper insight can help marriage counsellors and others to reconcile the parties and avoid breakdown. And he proposes ways in which the secular approach to divorce and the traditional Christian attitude might be harmonized.